MAKERS
of the
MUSLIM
WORLD

Ahmad ibn Hanbal

Series editor: Patricia Crone,
Institute for Advanced Study, Princeton

SELECTION OF TITLES IN THE MAKERS OF THE MUSLIM WORLD SERIES

For current information and details of other books in the
series, please visit www.oneworld-publications.com/
subjects/makers-of-muslim-world.htm

MAKERS
of the
MUSLIM
WORLD

Ahmad ibn Hanbal

CHRISTOPHER MELCHERT

ONEWORLD
OXFORD

AHMAD IBN HANBAL

Oneworld Publications
185 Banbury Road
Oxford OX2 7AR
England
www.oneworld-publications.com

ISBN 1–85168–407–7
978–1–85168–407–6

Typeset by Sparks, Oxford, UK
Cover and text design by Design Deluxe
Printed and bound in India by Replika Press Pvt. Ltd
on acid-free paper

CONTENTS

INTRODUCTION

This is a life of Ahmad ibn Hanbal, major advocate of Sunni theology, major collector and critic of hadith, and eponym of the Hanbali school of law. Sunni theology is still with us, Ahmad's great hadith collection, the *Musnad*, is available in multiple editions, and the Hanbali school is practically established in Saudi Arabia. Because he was on the winning side, Ahmad's life has unusual significance and can tell us more about Muslim values and experiences than that of almost any of his contemporaries. On the other hand, today's Sunni theology and Hanbali law are inevitably twentieth- or twenty-first-century versions, while the *Musnad* is read in a widely different context from the one in which it was composed. It is therefore particularly interesting how far Ahmad was aware of how his favorite projects were getting away from him: how, in his lifetime, Sunni theology, the collection and criticism of hadith, and Islamic law were developing in uncomfortable new ways. In many ways, Ahmad was not in the vanguard of the new Sunni synthesis but was the last of the rearguard, holding on to the ways of pious Muslims in the early period against urgings in favor of new, more accommodating ways.

One might well write a life of Ahmad by translating one of the medieval biographies. The first modern biography, published in 1897, was largely Walter Patton's retelling of the biography written by one of Ahmad's sons, Salih, which was known to Patton through the manuscript of a later compendium of biographies. It would be useful to students were such a translation available. My own knowledge of, for example, church history has depended heavily on translations from Greek and Latin. And I do not claim to know more than Ibn 'Asakir, Ibn al-Jawzi and al-Dhahabi.

The first disadvantage of translating a medieval biography is that it inevitably presents a medieval point of view. A full-time scholar has had the chance to develop a taste for such literature, but most readers would find it grotesque. For example, one chapter of Ibn al-Jawzi's biography is simply a list of the more than four hundred persons from whom Ahmad collected hadith. A proper analysis would easily exceed the limits of a normal biography (a recent scholarly treatment of just the 292 shaykhs who appear in the *Musnad* stretches to 420 pages) and I doubt would interest any but specialists. It would also be too long. The books in this series are about 40,000 words, whereas a translation of Dhahabi's would require a good 60,000 and Ibn al-Jawzi's over 150,000. Hence I make bold to compose a new biography.

A few words about usage. In modern Western scholarship, Ahmad is more often called *Ibn Hanbal*. He is sometimes called "Ibn Hanbal" in medieval Arabic sources, as well, though more usually, medieval sources refer to him as "Ahmad", and that is the custom I shall follow. ("Abu 'Abd Allah" is the standard designation in first-generation Hanbali works.) In this book, *Sunni* normally indicates what it did to Ahmad himself: the party that wanted Islamic law and theology to be based strictly on hadith as opposed to custom or rational speculation. It has a narrower range than that which it acquired in the century after Ahmad's death. *Renunciant* is my normal translation of the Arabic *zahid*, meaning someone who renounces this world and its comforts in favor of orienting himself towards God and the after-life. Islamicists have more often used *ascetic* but that has the disadvantages of having a technical sense in the sociology of religion (mainly in contrast to *mystic*) and of being a precise translation of *mujtahid* (a much less commonly used word in this part of the Islamic tradition) rather than *zahid*. Transliteration of Arabic follows the Library of Congress standard with the important exception that dots under consonants and macrons over vowels appear only in the index.

As a courtesy, I give years in split form: that is, the year of the Hijrah appears first, then the year of the Common Era; for example 241/855, the year of Ahmad's death. Centuries I give only after the Common Era; hence, "the eighth century" refers to 701–800 CE, corresponding roughly to AH 82–185. Hijri years, the natural preference of Arabic sources, follow the moon and therefore do not line up evenly with solar years. However, a given Hijri year indicates no less precisely when something happened than does a given year of the Common Era; simply guessing in which Common Era year a given event took place is not respectable scholarship.

References to the Prophet in Arabic sources are often followed by the words *salla Allah 'alayhi wa-sallam,* for which writers in English sometimes use the phrase "peace be upon him." I have omitted any such formula both out of courtesy to those Muslims who resent the expression when it is pronounced by non-Muslims and because "peace be upon him" is patently not a translation of the Arabic.

1

LIFE

Ahmad's ancestors were Arabs who participated in the Islamic conquests of the Sasanian Empire in the seventh and eighth centuries. Early biographies identify him as "Basran, Khurasani, Baghdadi." Basra, a city in southern Iraq, is recently famous as under the control of the British Army. Ahmad was Basran because his ancestors had settled there in the seventh century, when the Arabs first conquered Iraq. Khurasan was a faraway district comprising parts of present-day north-eastern Iran, Afghanistan, and Uzbekistan, which was conquered by Arabs operating from Basra. His grandfather, Hanbal, was governor of the city of Sarakhs. He played an important role in the Shiʿi revolution of 132/749 that ushered in the ʿAbbasid dynasty of caliphs. Ahmad's father, Muhammad, was born shortly after the revolution and became a soldier in the city of Marw, one of the four leading cities of Khurasan. His mother was Safiyah.

Ahmad was of pure Arab lineage, although the sources disagree as to his exact line before about the twelfth generation back (*Manaqib*, *bab* 2). Ahmad was reticent about his genealogy. When an Abu al-Nuʿman said to him, "Abu ʿAbd Allah, I have heard that you are of Arab ancestry," Ahmad replied, "Abu al-Nuʿman, we are poor people." He continued to repel Abu al-Nuʿman's inquiries and told him no more of his ancestry (*TMD* 5:258).

In the first two centuries, Islam and Arabism were so tightly identified that conversion to Islam required the convert almost to be adopted by an Arab. Muslims with Arab ancestors (in the male line) took pride in their superiority to those Muslims who lacked them. Yahya ibn Ma'in, whose ancestry was not Arab, remarked with relief that Ahmad never lorded his Arabness over others, nor even mentioned it (*TMD* 5:257–8). In classical Islamic law, pure Arabs had a few privileges over other Muslims, which Ahmad upheld. For example, a virgin daughter might normally be married to whomever her father chose; however, she had a veto if her proposed husband were of a demonstrably inferior social group, such as a non-Arab would be to an Arab. On the whole, though, Ahmad stood for ranking Muslims by their piety, not birth.

Ahmad was born in 164/780–1 but different sons quote him as specifying different months, Rabi' I or II (4 November/3 December or 4 December/1 January). His mother is said to have moved to Baghdad while carrying him, although in another version he was born in Marw and brought to Baghdad as an infant (*Manaqib*, 14–15 *12–15*; Khalili, 187–8). By one report, his father went to take part in holy war (*jihad*), presumably against the Byzantines to the northwest. His father died at thirty, when Ahmad was about three, so he was brought up by his mother. Ahmad grew up speaking Persian at home; a grandson recalled how when a cousin from Khurasan visited his father, Ahmad sat down with them for a fine meal and asked in Persian about his relations (*Manaqib*, 216–17 *296–7*).

Ahmad's mother fastened a pearl to each ear when he was a baby. Later, he took them off and sold them for thirty dirhams, the cost of a Spartan pilgrimage to Mecca (*Sirah*, 30, 33). There are several stories of conflicts with his mother over his determination to seek hadith (reports of what the Prophet and other early Muslims had said or done, thus showing the way to lead a God-pleasing life). She would withhold his clothes until the dawn call to prayer was heard, to prevent him leaving for the mosque any earlier. He also recollected sadly that he had not asked his mother's permission to walk to Kufa to seek hadith (*Sirah*, 33). In Islamic law, parental permission is needed to embark on the holy war but not to travel in quest of hadith.

Ahmad's basic education in reading, writing and arithmetic took place at a local *kuttab* (elementary school). There are stories of how illiterate women would ask the schoolmaster to send Ahmad ibn Hanbal to them to write letters to their husbands, campaigning with the caliph against the Byzantines. He would take their dictation with downcast eyes, so as not to look at women who were not close relatives, and never wrote down anything improper (*Manaqib*, 20 *22–3*).

He had an uncle in the caliphal bureaucracy, which is presumably one reason why, at fourteen, he moved from the *kuttab* to the *diwan*, an office of the government. Using family connections, he might have made his career as a scribe, but his piety got in the way. There are stories that his uncle asked him to convey reports on affairs at the capital that would eventually be passed to the caliph on the frontier, but Ahmad refused on seeing the caliph's courier, or even pitching his reports into the river (*Manaqib*, *bab* 3). It was pious not to have anything to do with the government, which was notorious for collecting taxes and expropriating land it should have left alone.

Ahmad also had (or developed) cultural objections to the scribal class. When someone wrote him to congratulate him on the birth of a child, he threw the letter down and said in disgust, "This is not a scholar's letter, or a traditionist's, but a scribe's" (*Manaqib*, 303 *409*). The scribes cultivated a clever rhetorical style that set them apart from the common people but seemed frivolous to the serious-minded Ahmad. (However, Ahmad is said to have taken care to speak with all the correct case endings and to have beaten a daughter who did not [IAY, 1:7; *Manaqib*, 307 *414*].)

RELIGIOUS KNOWLEDGE

Ahmad began to seek hadith in 179/795–6, when he was fifteen years old (he is quoted as saying "when I was sixteen" but this presumably meant in his sixteenth year; *Manaqib*, *bab* 4). This was the start of his life's work. His quest would, over the next twenty-five years, take him to Kufa, Wasit and Basra in Iraq, to Mecca and Yemen, to the Byzantine border at Tarsus and to Homs and Damascus in Syria. His travels will be covered further in Chapter 2, *Hadith*.

When Ahmad was twenty-eight or thirty (that is, in 192/807–8 or 194/809–10), the famous jurisprudent al-Shafi'i (died Old Cairo, 204/820) is said to have suggested to the caliph al-Amin that he be appointed qadi for Yemen, "since you like going to 'Abd al-Razzaq and will judge justly." However, Ahmad wanted nothing to do with the judgeship and told Shafi'i he would never see him again if he said any more about it (*TMD* 5:273–4). He had two powerful objections to being a qadi. First, he would not wish to identify himself with the ruling power (in the early ninth century, qadis were thought to judge as deputies of the caliph himself). Second, he would not wish to renounce the prerogative of answering questions cautiously, to say "I don't know" or "I hope there is no harm in it," rather than having to make decisions with immediate and often irrevocable consequences. Unfortunately, the story is less likely to be an actual incident in Ahmad's life than a later fiction to illustrate his piety and Shafi'i's respect for him.

FAMILY MAN

Ahmad did not marry or occupy himself with making money until he was past the age of forty and had got the knowledge he wanted. We are told that he was precisely forty at the time of his first marriage, which means he married in 204/819–20. His wife was an 'Abbasah bint al-Fadl, of Arab lineage. She gave birth to a son, Salih, who grew up to be Ahmad's biographer, a collector of his opinions, and a qadi. Then she died (IAY, 2:49; *Manaqib*, 298 *402*).

Ahmad next married his paternal cousin, Rayhanah, who was one-eyed. She gave birth to a son, 'Abd Allah, who grew up to be the main collector of Ahmad's opinions and hadith (IAY, 2:49; *Manaqib*, 299 *403*), before she in her turn died. Rayhanah may have been a concubine, whom Ahmad bought, with his wife's permission, for the sake of offspring (*Manaqib*, 177 *243*). However, Ahmad is also reported to have told a disciple, 'Salih's mother lived with me for thirty years without our disagreeing over a single word" (*Manaqib*, 298–9 *402–3*). If she was with him for thirty years, she must have died about 234/848–9, whereas 'Abd Allah is said to have been born in 213/828–9 (*TB* 9:376). Therefore, it seems likely that Ahmad's household at some point included either two wives or a wife and a concubine.

Then Ahmad bought Husn, who gave birth to several children: Umm 'Ali Zaynab, a daughter (perhaps also called Fatimah – girls might bear two names), twins al-Hasan and al-Husayn, who died shortly after birth, al-Hasan and Muhammad, who lived to be around 40 years old, and finally Sa'id, who grew up to become a deputy qadi in Kufa (IAY, 2:49; *Manaqib*, 307 *414*).

For years, I have collected references to the sources of income of Muslim men of religion. The one that comes up most often is trade; for example, Ahmad's shaykh, Abu 'Asim al-Nabil (died Basra, 212/828?), was a silk trader (*TI* 15:192). The second most common is income from rents. Ahmad's principal source of income seems to have been renting out the property he inherited from his father: one shop brought in three dirhams a month (*Hilyah* 9:179). A collection of shops is said to have yielded seventeen dirhams a month in the 220s/ mid-830s–40s (Ibn Kathir, 10:337). He occasionally sold items made by his womenfolk, mainly spun yarn and woven cloth (*Sirah*, 42) and sometimes accepted a government stipend (*'ata'*) as an Arab and a soldier's son (*Siyar* 11:320). He also went out to glean (*Siyar* 11:320).

Ahmad seems to have been continually short of cash. A bookseller relates getting four or five dirhams from a person who said it was half of everything he owned. The bookseller went on to Ahmad, who gave him four dirhams, with the comment that it was *all* he owned. There are several other stories in which he gives away all he owns, in the form of four or five dirhams (*Manaqib*, 240 324–5). He is reported to have been overjoyed when one of his tenants came to him with one and a half dirhams: "I supposed that he had assigned it to some pressing need" (*Manaqib*, 225 307).

Ahmad's house was probably divided into sections around a central courtyard. Ahmad's sons lived there even after they married. It had a well, as is shown by the tale of Abu al-Fawaris, who rented a property from Ahmad. One day, Ahmad told him that the boy had thrown a set of shears down the well. (Parents know how these things happen.) Abu al-Fawaris went down to retrieve them, so Ahmad instructed his grocer to give him half a dirham. Ahmad had an account with this grocer and evidently used him as banker. Abu al-Fawaris refused to take half a dirham for so small a job, so Ahmad excused him of three months' rent (*Siyar* 11:219).

AHMAD'S CHARACTER

Leading features of Ahmad's piety were his unremitting seriousness and inattention to the world around him. One disciple recalled how Ahmad would sit in silence while those around him chatted about mundane subjects, becoming voluble only when "knowledge" (meaning hadith) came into the conversation (*Hilyah* 9:164). In another story, Ahmad was walking with his leading disciple Abu Bakr al-Marrudhi, leaning on his arm. They came across a woman carrying a sort of lute, which Marrudhi took from her, smashed, and trampled underfoot (music being thought to be a reprehensible distraction from the proper occupations of a Muslim), while Ahmad stood by, looking at the ground. Word of the incident spread and eventually came back to the house. Ahmad declared that only at that moment had he learnt what Marrudhi had done (*Manaqib*, 285 *381*).

Ahmad wanted to spread the truth, but he had no ambitions for personal honor and fame. Although he sat in the mosque after the afternoon prayer, ready to offer judicial opinions (*fatwas*), he would not speak unless asked a question (*Siyar* 11:217). An uncle came to visit him and found him lying with his hand under his cheek. The uncle said, "Nephew, what is this gloom? What is this sadness?" Ahmad raised his head and said, "Uncle, blessed is he whose renown God has extinguished" (*Jarh* 1:306). After the abolition of the Inquisition (of which more below), he became the most famous man in Baghdad. "I want to die," he told his son 'Abd Allah:

> This matter is more severe than that. That was the trial of flogging and imprisonment, which I could bear. This is the trial of the world. (*Siyar* 11:215) ... I wish I were in a gorge of Mecca and so unknown. I have been tried by fame. I wish for death morning and evening. (*Siyar* 11:216)

There are some stories to relate of Ahmad's generosity and kindness. The most touching picture is of him during a journey to meet the caliph in Samarra, where he dreaded to go. As he sat by the roadside to eat some bread a dog appeared, sat opposite Ahmad and wagged its tail. So Ahmad threw a morsel to the dog, ate one himself, then threw another to the dog. His disciple, Marrudhi, tried to chase the dog away but noticed that Ahmad was red with embarrassment. "Leave him alone," he said, "for Ibn 'Abbas said they were evil spirits," meaning it might retaliate by the evil eye (*Manaqib*, 241–2 *326*). When his grandsons visited, on Fridays, it is reported that Ahmad asked his agent to give them two pieces of silver each (*Siyar* 11:217). His concubine was once overheard complaining that they were always straitened whereas they ate and did all sorts of things "over at Salih's." Ahmad simply said to her, "Say what is good" (or be quiet). Then he went out with a son, who began to cry. "What do you want?" Ahmad asked him. "Raisins," he said. So Ahmad sent him to the grocer to buy some (*Manaqib*, 247 *332–3*).

Regrettably, there are no stories of kindness to non-Sunni enemies or non-Muslims. "Whenever Ahmad saw a Christian, he closed his eyes. He was asked about that and said, 'I cannot look at someone who has lied about God and lied to him" (IAY, 1:12). "He loved in God and hated in God," recalled Marrudhi. "In matters of religion, his anger became intense. He put up with nuisances from the neighbours" (*Siyar* 11:221).

THE INQUISITION

The Inquisition, which established Ahmad's fame, was about the demand for agreement with the doctrine that the Qur'an was created, not eternal. Caliph al-Ma'mun (reigned 198–218/813–33) proclaimed this doctrine in 212/827, at the same time as he announced that 'Ali was the best of people after the Prophet, and hence better than the first three caliphs before him, Abu Bakr, 'Umar, and 'Uthman (Tabari, 3:1099). The connection between Qur'an and 'Ali was presumably the emphasis on persons as the locus of authority – persons such as the caliph but not such as the amorphous body of self-proclaimed experts like Ahmad ibn Hanbal and his fellow hadith students.

In modern scholarship, the idea that the Qur'an was created has continually been associated with the Mu'tazilah. However, the person most often associated with the doctrine of the created Qur'an in our sources is Bishr al-Marisi (died 218/833–4?), who is known to have been a student of Hanafi law but not of Mu'tazilism. He was arrested and, before a crowd, required to renounce this doctrine some time in 201–3/817–19, when Baghdad was briefly held by the anti-caliph, Ibrahim ibn al-Mahdi (died 224/839), but managed to escape through a side door (Waki', 3:270). The Mu'tazilah agreed that God must have created the Qur'an, but it was not originally or mainly their doctrine that Ma'mun strove to establish. Ahmad used the term "Jahmi" not "Mu'tazili" to refer to those who upheld the createdness of the Qur'an.

Both sides engaged in vigorous back-projection of their positions. For example, Abu Hanifah's grandson is said to have assured Ma'mun that he, his father, and his grandfather all believed the Qur'an was created (TB 6:245). On the other side, early Hanbali sources assert that Malik ibn Anas, the great Medinan jurisprudent (died 179/795), called for the flogging of anyone who said the Qur'an was created and then his imprisonment until he repented (Sirah, 67; Sunnah, 5 11). Another source relates that one of Ahmad's most important disciples had someone ask Ibn Abi 'Alqamah of Medina (died 253/867?) what the people of Medina said about the pronunciation of the Qur'an (some would-be Sunni theologians having allowed that one's pronunciation of the Qur'an was created, even if the Qur'an itself was not). Ibn Abi 'Alqamah answered that he had not heard any discussion of the Qur'an until 209/824–5, which casts doubt on Malik's actually having expressed any opinion at all (TI 19:360–1).

No practical consequences arose from the caliph's endorsement of the doctrine that the Qur'an was created until 218/833, when he sent letters to the provinces instructing that the local men of religion be questioned to make sure they subscribed to this doctrine (Tabari, 3:1112–34). The letters to the Baghdad prefect of police are quoted in full by the historian al-Tabari and they make Ma'mun's motives clear. First, Ma'mun asserts it is his duty as caliph to determine and uphold religious orthodoxy. Second, he asserts that the doctrine of the self-proclaimed Sunni party, which denied that the Qur'an was created and had appeared in time, was analogous to what the Nazarenes (Christians) said about Jesus the son of Mary. We should probably take him at his word. The modern proposal that he wanted the Qur'an to be created so he could more easily set aside the Qur'anic rules in favor of his own seems especially unlikely (Watt, 179). The caliph's allies, the Mu'tazilah, were (with the Khawarij) the leading advocates of a law based on the Qur'an, whereas it was Ma'mun's Sunni opponents who continually set aside the apparent meaning of the Qur'an for something else (mainly hadith).

If the created nature of the Qur'an was a doctrine without practical consequence, why did the Sunnis bother to oppose him? To some extent, they did fear that the caliph meant to set aside the Qur'an. One of Ahmad's shaykhs, Hajjaj al-A'war (died 206/821–2), was quoted as saying that what they meant by calling the Qur'an created was that it was nothing (Sunnah, 14 19–20). However, their main reason was probably the mirror image of the caliph's; that is, to defend their authority to define orthodoxy. Naturally, they put it in less self-serving terms: they found no discussion of the created nature of the Qur'an in hadith, the body of evidence in which they were expert, and would not accord equal authority to subtle theological reasoning.

First, a group of seven was singled out and made to testify publicly that the Qur'an was created. This group included Abu Khaythamah and Yahya ibn Ma'in, companions with whom Ahmad had sought hadith. When all seven had testified, a larger group, which included Ahmad, was assembled and ordered to make the same declaration. The caliph declared that no one who refused to testify that the Qur'an was created was fit to be employed as a witness-notary in court, to give juridical opinions, or to relate hadith. Some testified immediately while some offered compromises ("We do whatever the caliph tells us to" or "The Qur'an is the speech of God, who is the creator") but made full testaments after further threats. Only two, Ahmad ibn Hanbal and another traditionist, Muhammad ibn Nuh, held out. They were then sent, in chains, to the Byzantine border to be interrogated under the caliph's personal supervision.

However, the caliph died suddenly and so Ahmad and Muhammad were sent back to Baghdad. Muhammad ibn Nuh died on the way but Ahmad was imprisoned. About two years later, he was brought before the new caliph, al-Mu'tasim (reigned 218–27/833–42), and bidden anew to testify that the Qur'an was created. There are various accounts of the ensuing debate between Ahmad and the caliph's representatives, such as the vizier, Ibn Abi Duwad. The friendly Hanbali accounts naturally tend to be fuller but all of them point to Ahmad's refusal to debate at the level of the caliph's representatives. The fact of this refusal has different connotations in different accounts. The Mu'tazili tradition stresses Ahmad's admitted incompetence in *kalam* (dialectical theology; for example, Ibn al-Murtada, 125), whereas the Hanbali stresses the rationalists' inability to come up with arguments from the Qur'an and hadith (for example, Hanbal, 43–61).

After three days of futile debate, the exasperated caliph ordered that Ahmad be flogged until he testified. His outer clothing was removed, baring his back, and he was forced to stand up against a rack and grasp two projections. A hundred and fifty floggers were assembled, each of whom would run up, strike twice, then retreat, to be followed by another (Hanbal, 62; *TMD* 5:312–13). Thirty-odd lashes (accounts vary) produced a result.

There are discrepancies between the friendly and hostile accounts. According to the latter, Ahmad ultimately confessed and was released (Hinds) whereas the Hanbali sources stress Ahmad's loss of consciousness and the caliph's fear of popular rioting should Ahmad die under the lash. Ahmad is quoted as saying:

> I lost consciousness and did not regain it until I was in a chamber, released from my bonds (*Sirah*, 63).
>
> I lost consciousness and relaxed. When I sensed that I was dying – as if I were afraid of that – at that point, he ordered me released. I was unconscious of that. I did not regain consciousness until I was in a chamber, released from my bonds. (Hanbal, 62–3)

We come close to a confession in one friendly account, according to which Ahmad recited the Qur'anic verses "Say, he is God, one" and "There is no god but God," whereupon a courtier announced, "O Commander of the Faithful, he has said as you say" and the caliph ordered his release (*Hilyah* 9:206). The Hanbali tradition itself records uncertainty among his followers as to Ahmad's precise doctrine in the years immediately after his release (*Sunnah*, 61 70). It seems probable that he said something in his agony, conceivable that it was something ambiguous that the anxious court took as the proper testimony.

The sources (all friendly, now, for the hostile sources show no further interest in Ahmad's career) also disagree about what went on during the next ten years or so. One source admits uncertainty as to chronology (Hanbal, 79). To me, four developments stand out. First, a riot broke out scarcely ten days after the death of Mu'tasim and the accession of his son, al-Wathiq (reigned 227–32/842–7). The crowd beat and humiliated two Jahmiyah at the mosque in Rusafah, one of the four main districts of Baghdad, and then went on to the personal mosque of the local qadi to erase a slogan he had written mentioning the created nature of the Qur'an. A servant of the qadi's saw them and fired arrows at them, upon which they attacked his house, burned down the door, and pillaged the house while the qadi fled (*TB* 9:243).

Second, a messenger came to Ahmad in the middle of the night to tell him the caliph had not forgotten him. "Let no one meet with you and do not live in a territory or city that I am in. Go where you like in God's earth" (Hanbal, 83–4). Presumably this message was sent from heightened fear of popular rebellion. Ahmad immediately went into hiding. Ibrahim ibn Hani' recalled how he stayed with him for three days, then bade him find him another place of refuge, just as the Prophet himself had taken refuge from his persecutors in a cave for just three days before moving on (IAY, 1:97). After some time, a few months or a year, Ahmad furtively returned to his house, but it is uncertain whether he ever again emerged from it, even to attend Friday prayer.

Third, a man named Ahmad ibn Nasr led an abortive revolt against the caliph in 231/846. He was beheaded and his body and head displayed in different cities together with inscriptions re-asserting the created nature of the Qur'an (*TB* 5:174–80). Some Baghdadi jurisprudents asked Ahmad if they should no longer recognize Wathiq's authority. Ahmad told them that they were obliged to repudiate him in their hearts but should not openly disobey or cause strife among Muslims (Hanbal, 81–2).

Last, at some point Ahmad swore not to relate any more hadith. I wish one of Ahmad's previous biographers, unconstrained by word limits, had gathered and evaluated all the various accounts; unfortunately, none has. To me it seems most likely that he renounced the relation of hadith of his own volition on 26 Sha'ban 227/10 June 842, after a qadi had denounced him to Wathiq, but before receiving any command so to cease (*Manaqib*, 348 *471*). Fear of the caliph's violence may have been significant, but another motivation would have been to avoid the public attention that came with relating hadith and thus the temptation to pride. Ahmad's renunciant contemporary Bishr al-Hafi (died Baghdad, 227/841), much quoted by the next generation of Hanabilah, prayed to God to forgive him every step he had taken in quest of hadith (*TB* 4:344–5). Bishr is quoted as explaining that he did not relate hadith because he wanted to "and whenever I desire something, I renounce it" (*TB* 7:70). Marrudhi quoted Ahmad, on being told that somebody wanted to meet him, as saying "I have taken rest. I have had no repose except since I swore not to relate hadith. Would that they left us [alone]. The way is what Bishr ibn al-Harith followed" (*Siyar* 11:216).

Al-Mutawakkil, who succeeded Wathiq in 232/847, began to dismantle the Inquisition by stages. The first positive step came two years later, when he paid some famous jurisprudents and traditionists to travel to Baghdad and to his capital, Samarra, some 135 kilometers distant, to preach against the theologians who had inspired the Inquisition (but at the same time, apparently, to exalt him and his dynasty). Three years on, he dismissed Ibn Abi Duwad and his son, and had Ahmad ibn Nasr's head and body taken down. To mark his full embrace of Sunnism as orthodoxy, he summoned Ahmad to Samarra for an audience and to teach hadith to one of his sons, the future caliph al-Mu'tazz. Ahmad had long resolved to have nothing to

do with rulers and patronage and moreover was not supposed
to relate hadith to anyone, so Mutawakkil's attentions were
wholly repugnant.

The story of Ahmad's trip to Samarra and his two-week
sojourn there is told in loving detail, especially the tales of the
caliph's blandishments and Ahmad's steadfast refusal to enjoy
anything he offered. Before entering the caliph's presence, he
was directed to put off his customary clothing, rough but pure
white, in favor of black, the color of the 'Abbasid dynasty. He
stood unmoving while a servant dressed him. Later, when the
caliph had given up and allowed him and his party to return
to the house provided for them, he threw off his new black
clothing and wept. "I have kept safe from them for sixty years,"
he lamented, "only to be tried by them at the end of my life"
(*Sirah*, 102).

Once back in Baghdad, there were frequent visits from the
caliph's agents and regular presents from the caliph. Ahmad
was willing to dictate a letter to the vizier's brother, evaluat-
ing ten candidates for judgeships (*Manaqib*, 183–5 251–2) but
otherwise wanted nothing to do with salutations or presents.
However, his sons and uncle were willing to accept them. Salih
remonstrated with him:

> Nobody is needier or has a better excuse than I. I used to
> complain to you and you would say, "Your affair is involved with
> mine. Perhaps God will release me from this knot." You used to
> pray for me, so now I hope that God has answered you.

Ahmad would hear none of it and ordered the door to Salih's
section of the house to be blocked (*Sirah*, 111). Once, when
he had not eaten for three days, he borrowed some flour of a
friend. When he was served bread, he asked how they had managed to bake it so quickly. When they told him they had used
Salih's oven, as it was hot, Ahmad refused to eat (*TMD* 5:302).

He even took to praying in a different mosque from the rest of the family (*Sirah*, 112).

THE END

Four years after the end of the Inquisition and forty days after the birth of his youngest son, Sa'id, Ahmad developed a fever and died ten days later. During his final illness, helped by his son Salih, he continued to stand to pray and did not moan until the last night. This lack of moaning had a ritual character, for near the beginning of his illness he had asked Salih to read the hadith report in which Tawus, a famous Yemeni Follower, expressed a dislike for moaning when one was ill (*Sirah*, 127). Around the house, the streets filled up with weeping crowds.

Ahmad left less than a dirham in cash and asked that it be spent atoning for a vow he thought he had failed to keep (*Zuhd*, 187 *234*). It was reported that on the day of his death, the ground shook in 'Abadan, a favorite retreat of renunciants some five hundred kilometers from Baghdad (*TMD* 5:313). Salih fully expected to perform the funeral prayer but at the last moment he was forcibly prevented, in favor of the governor of Baghdad (*Sirah*, 129). Various fantastic numbers are said to have attended the funeral: 2.5 million, 1.8 million (not counting those in boats), 1.5 million, 1 million or 800,000 men and 60,000 women. Ten or, alternatively, twenty thousand Jews, Christians, and Magians are said to have converted to Islam that day (*Jarh* 1:312; *TMD* 5:330–5; *Siyar* 11:339–40, 343).

Modern historians have interpreted the Inquisition as a turning point in Islamic history. Sunni Muslims have usually thought it a wrong turn, happily reversed before too long. A ninth-century traditionist singled out the three greatest caliphs: "Abu Bakr fought the apostates, 'Umar ibn 'Abd al-'Aziz established the equity court, and al-Mutawakkil returned the people to orthodoxy" (Waki', 3:180). It is surprising to see Mutawakkil put above 'Umar, 'Uthman, and 'Ali, but perhaps the speaker was seeking an appointment. Western historians have noticed lasting changes. H. A. R. Gibb considered the end of the Inquisition the decisive moment when the Muslims repudiated the Hellenistic tradition of the Middle East (Gibb, 19). Probably more scholars would now agree with Martin Hinds, that it represented, more modestly, repudiation of the Mu'tazilah and their style of theology in favor of Sunnism and the repudiation of the caliph as the arbiter of orthodoxy. The Inquisition was not the last time Muslims would persecute other Muslims for wrong beliefs, but henceforward it would not be the caliph persecuting in his own name, on his personal and sole responsibility for maintaining correct belief, but rather the caliph or other prince would act as the agent of the ulema, the learned men of the community.

Ahmad would probably have agreed with this diminution of caliphal pretensions but who could advise the caliph? Yahya ibn Ma'in and 'Ali ibn al-Madini collected hadith alongside Ahmad in their youth and with him became major hadith experts in maturity, but both testified in 218/833 that the Qur'an was created. Ahmad would have nothing more to do with either of them. Yahya once visited him when he was ill but Ahmad turned his face to the wall and would not speak to him. Yahya pleaded, giving the example of someone earlier, who had been forced to embrace heresy. After he left, Ahmad dismissed his argument on the grounds that that man had embraced heresy only when he was beaten whereas Yahya had merely been threatened (*Manaqib*, 389 523–4). However, despite Ahmad's fame and prestige as a hadith critic and upholder of orthodoxy, the reputations of Yahya ibn Ma'in and 'Ali ibn al-Madini suffered little. Thanks to 'Abd Allah, some of their hadith even found its way into the *Musnad*. The future was in the hands of people who respected Ahmad but also, inevitably, in the hands of people a good deal less personally heroic.

HADITH

"Hadith" means the short reports (or a single report – the Arabic word is used both ways) of what the Prophet or some early authoritative teacher said. Ahmad's major life-work was to collect and sort hadith and his chief literary monument is the *Musnad,* a massive collection. In our time, his name is perhaps best known by the school of law named after him; in his own time, he was hugely admired for standing up at the Inquisition. He had no intention of founding a school based on his opinions, for valid opinions were those based on the Qur'an and the hadith; he believed his opinions were authoritative only in so far as they were scrupulously based on them. In the Inquisition, his position was that no one should affirm the created nature of the Qur'an just because there was nothing in the hadith about it. The hadith were the main thing. Tenth-century writers classed Ahmad primarily as a collector and critic of hadith and only secondarily as a jurisprudent.

THE CHARACTER OF HADITH

A hadith report normally comes in two parts: the *matn* (main part) is what the Prophet or other authority said and the *isnad* (support) is the chain of authorities by which it has reached the collector. The *isnad* is proof that the report was not made up somewhere along the way and historically projected onto a venerable authority of the past. (Hadith reports were once called "traditions," by analogy with pre-literary oral reports of what Jesus said. Hadith is now the standard term but I still use "traditionist" for someone who collects hadith, rather than the Arabic *muhaddith* or, as was normal in Ahmad's day, *sahib al-hadith*.)

Later writers distinguish between *hadith,* which went back to the Prophet, and *athar*, which went back to other early Muslims, but Ahmad uses the terms interchangeably. An example of a hadith report going back to the Prophet is below. This example is from Ahmad's book *al-Zuhd* and is not in the *Musnad*; however, the *Musnad* has other similar hadith about Yahya:

> There related to us 'Abd Allah: there related to me my father [that is, Ahmad]: there related to us Ibn 'Uyaynah from 'Amr from Yahya ibn Ja'dah from the Prophet: he said, Yahya ibn Zakariya [John the Baptist] never had a sinful thought, nor did a woman ever disturb his breast.

> (*Zuhd*, 76 97)

(For convenience, I shall in future replace "There related to us", "from", and so on with the symbol <.) An example of a hadith report going back only to a Companion is:

> 'Abd Allah < his father < Wahb ibn Jarir < his father < Mansur ibn Zadhan < Sa'id ibn Abi Burdah < his father < Abu Musa: "These dirhams and dinars destroyed those who came before you and I do not see but that they are destroying you".

> (Presumably from a sermon; *Zuhd*, 199 247)

Sometimes the authority quoted is a prophet who pre-dates Muhammad and normally is to do with encouragements to piety rather than establishing a point of law. For example:

'Abd Allah < his father < Sufyan (i.e. ibn 'Uyaynah) < Abu
Sinan < Abu al-Hudhayl: 'Isa (Jesus) brought forth a man who
had committed adultery and ordered them to stone him. He
told them, "Let no man stone him who has done what he has
done." They threw down the stones from their hands except for
Yahya ibn Zakariya.

(*Zuhd*, 76 97)

This is plainly an Islamic version of the story of the woman
taken in adultery (John 8:3–11). It makes the same point about
hypocrisy as does the New Testament, but, in distinctively
Islamic fashion, the prophets uphold justice (an adulterer
should be stoned, according to the law) above repentance and
the remission of sin.

Sometimes either Muhammad or an earlier prophet quotes
God. For example:

'Abd Allah < his father < 'Abd al-Razzaq and 'Abd al-A'la
(both) < Ma'mar < al-Zuhri < Sa'id < the Messenger of God:
"Every part of a person's ritual worship [*kullu 'amal ibn Adam*] is
for him except fasting, fasting being for me".

(*Musnad* 2:273 13:127)

This is sometimes called a *hadith qudsi*. The obvious application of this particular hadith is to encourage fasting by daylight
during the month of Ramadan. Today, Muslims praise the Ramadan fast as a means of promoting physical health and sympathy
with the poor, but medieval writers saw it as a uniquely private
act of obedience: unlike the ritual prayer, paying the alms tax,
and making the pilgrimage, fasting does not consist of any visible action, so only God and the individual concerned know
whether he has fulfilled his duty.

The hadith I have just quoted mainly concern the life of piety
but the last has a more particularly legal application, as well.

I came across it in a handbook of Shafi'i law, in a discussion of whether it is more virtuous to pray or fast. (It does not appear in the *Musnad* with this *isnad*.) I shall write more about the significance of the law in the next chapter, but here, suffice it to say that for Ahmad, the law was the most important expression of Islamic faithfulness (as in Rabbinic Judaism).

In Ahmad's day, the spectrum of Islamic opinion on the significance of the hadith ran, almost as in ours, from those who thought that the hadith were an indispensable, even supremely important indicator of God's will (that is, the law), to those who thought that Muslims could work out how to lead God-pleasing lives without them. Ahmad lay at the Sunni extreme in favor of hadith. In his view, a thorough knowledge of the Qur'an was good and necessary but far from sufficient; thorough acquaintance with theological reasoning was not even good and necessary. Knowing the hadith was the foremost thing. The first step was to collect them: to listen to various masters, writing down and memorizing hadith that they had heard in their youth.

THE AGE FOR COLLECTING HADITH

Ahmad began his life's work of seeking hadith in 179/795–6, when he was fifteen years old. This seems to have been a fairly usual age for starting; an age when a boy had memorized the Qur'an and mastered reading and arithmetic (particularly the calculation of inheritance shares). Ahmad's younger contemporaries Bukhari (died 256/870) and Muslim (died 261/875) first heard hadith at eleven and fourteen respectively. During the ninth and tenth centuries the trend was towards collecting hadith at an earlier and earlier age; by the eleventh century, it was normal to hear hadith when just five or six years old.

A boy's written notes (probably really prepared by a servant) were signed by the aged traditionist who had dictated
the hadith they recorded. If a boy of five was unable quite to
understand his notes, he could return to them later, memorize
what was there, and say, near the end of his life, when he in his
turn dictated hadith, that he was passing them on exactly as
they had been passed to him.

In Ahmad's time, there was still doubt as to whether someone could legitimately relate what he had heard as a very young
boy. At fifteen, he might be assumed to be at an age when he
could begin to understand the legal implications of the hadith.
Ahmad himself is quoted as saying that he did not understand
all he heard from his first shaykh in hadith, Hushaym ibn Bashir
(died 183/799; *Hilyah* 9:164). The prominent Basran Qur'an
reciter, Ya'qub al-Hadrami (died 205/820–1), was disparaged
for relating hadith that he had heard at an early age (Ibn Sa'd,
7/2:55 *7:304*). Ahmad's contemporary, Ishaq ibn Rahawayh
(died 238/853?), heard hadith from Ibn al-Mubarak (whom
Ahmad just missed) but stopped relating hadith he had heard
from him because of his youth at the time (*Lisan* 1:277). A
Baghdadi hadith expert who flourished in the later ninth century said, "The people of Basra write at ten, the people of Kufa
at twenty, and the people of Syria at thirty," meaning that these
were the ages from which they took down hadith (*Muhaddith*,
187). Ahmad defended his hearing hadith before he was fifteen,
citing the examples of his shaykhs Sufyan ibn 'Uyaynah (died
198/814), Waki' (died 196/811–12?) and others ('Al., 449).
Sufyan's case shows the doubts felt in the eighth century about
hearing hadith at a very young age. Reports vary as to just how
young he was when he first heard hadith, from seven to fifteen
(*Siyar* 8:404, 408). At sixteen, he met the famous traditionist
al-Zuhri (died 125/742–3?), which provoked al-Zuhri to comment that he had never seen anyone younger than he collecting

hadith (*TB* 9:176). The important Meccan jurisprudent Ibn Jurayj (died 150/767–8?) thought Waki', at eighteen, was very young to be collecting hadith (*Kifayah, ma ja'a fi sihhat sama' al-saghir*). Therefore, it cannot have been normal, in the eighth century, to hear hadith before fifteen.

In the tenth and eleventh centuries, the argument for hearing hadith at a very early age that seems to have won the day was that many, many hadith reports are authenticated by *isnads* that end with some Follower < some Companion < the Prophet, where the Companion was only five years old at the Prophet's death. If everyone followed Ishaq and others in disregarding what was heard at an early age, a great many hadith would have to be discarded.

WRITING DOWN HADITH

The acceptance of learning hadith at five or six probably had something to do with the balance between writing down and memorizing. In the eighth century, when hearing hadith before fifteen was unusual, written notes were also suspect. It seems to have been widely feared that a body of hadith in writing would challenge the Qur'an's status as the sole Islamic Scripture. Ahmad's *Musnad* includes several versions of the hadith report in which the Prophet said, "Do not write anything of me except the Qur'an. Whoever writes anything of me besides the Qur'an, let him erase it" (*Musnad* 3:12 *17:149*, etc.). Ahmad quoted the Companion al-Dahhak as warning, "Do not take up books (*kararis*) for hadith as you do for copies of the Qur'an" ("*Ilal* 1:217 *1:97*). In similar fashion, for centuries Jewish Rabbis preferred to maintain the oral law separate from the written Torah, memorizing and dictating it but not writing it down. Ahmad quoted this analysis of his own shaykh, the

Basran Isma'il ibn 'Ulayyah (died 193/809?): "They used to dislike writing because those before you took up books and were pleased by them. They used to dislike to be distracted by them from the Qur'an" (*'Ilal* 2:388 *1:339*). "Those before you" normally refers to Jews and Christians who had fallen into error, presumably through spending too much time with books other than Scripture.

Another reason for maintaining oral transmission was to maintain the power and prestige of teachers. Of course, teachers will never be so blatantly self-serving as to justify oral transmission by its benefit to themselves: they will explain that their material cannot be properly understood without an oral commentary from a qualified teacher. Plato complained that a living teacher could answer questions whereas, if a student failed to understand a written text, all the text could do was to say the same thing over and over again, like an idiot. Reputable colleges and universities still refuse to grant a degree merely for proof that someone has read a given set of books: students must spend time with teachers, receiving oral instruction. When they are dealing with sacred knowledge, such as hadith, teachers will all the more insist on controlling access to their material.

There is a great deal of evidence of anxiety not to spread knowledge of the hadith too widely. The Basran, Abu Qilabah (died 104/722–3), said, "Relate hadith only to one who recognizes it, for it will only harm one who does not recognize it, not help him" (*Zuhd*, 303 *368*). The famous Kufan, al-A'mash (died 148/765–6?), would not relate hadith to some people. A companion reproached him: "Abu Muhammad, why don't you relate hadith to these poor people?" Al-A'mash replied, "Who hangs pearls on swine?" (*Hilyah* 5:52). We not rarely read of a heretic expelled from a particular circle, as a way of preserving this precious, sacred material. Some early figures were notoriously slow to relate what they knew. (Occasionally, it seems, this had to do with driving up the price, as traditionists took to accepting gifts for relating hadith.) For non-religious texts, there was, naturally, less fear that copies might get into the wrong hands, so written transmission was always much more acceptable in literature and the sciences (medicine, astronomy, mathematics, etc.). Ahmad himself approved of relating hadith to anyone. When a disciple told him there were some tradition-ists to whom one should relate nothing, he merely said, "Hadith lead to nothing but good" (Ibn Hani', 2:165).

To keep hadith from falling into the wrong hands, famous tra-ditionists sometimes required letters of recommendation from previous shaykhs. Ahmad went to Husayn al-Ju'fi with such a letter but Husayn had already heard of him and said a recom-mendation was not necessary (Manaqib, 72 92). Ahmad recalled that the Yemeni, Ibrahim ibn 'Aqil, was notably stingy:

> No one could get to him. So I stayed at his door in Yemen a day or two until I got to him. He related to me two hadith reports. He had the hadith of Wahb ibn Jarir. I never got to hear them on account of his stinginess. Isma'il ibn 'Abd al-Karim would not relate them to us because he (Ibrahim ibn 'Aqil) was alive, so I never heard them from anyone.

(Manaqib, 29 34–5).

The early view was that face-to-face speaking and listening ensured accurate transmission: notes were unreliable. Islamic judicial procedure strongly emphasizes oaths rather than docu-ments as evidence of contracts. The famous Kufan traditionist, al-Sha'bi (died after 100/718), is said to have told people to relate hadith from their notebooks "only if you remember it – people write what they please and seal what they please" (Hilyah 4:314). When somebody related to Isma'il ibn 'Ulayyah a hadith report of the Prophet that called for writing down whatever he said, Isma'il shook his garment, as though to clear the air, and said repeatedly, "I take refuge with God from lying and the people who lie" (*'Ilal* 1:245 *1:105*). Ahmad's shaykh 'Abd al-Rahman ibn Mahdi (died 198/814), also of Basra, was never seen with a notebook (*TB* 10:247) and Sufyan ibn 'Uyaynah either had no books or declared that his memory was more reliable than his notes (*TB* 9:179; *Tahdhib* 4:121).

Several modern Muslim scholars have assiduously collected references to writing down hadith in the seventh and eighth centuries, to prove that written notes were always normal and hence the transmission of the hadith was always reliable. Some of these stories seem fairly tortuous and unbelievable. For example, a letter from the Prophet Muhammad to 'Amr ibn Hazm was tied to the quiver of the second caliph 'Umar ibn al-Khattab, then copied by Abu Bakr ibn 'Ubayd Allah ibn 'Abd Allah ibn 'Umar, who transmitted it in writing to 'Ikrimah ibn Khalid, who transmitted it orally to Ibn Jurayj, who transmitted it orally to Hajjaj, who finally communicated it to Ibn Zanjawayh, the ninth-century source for this report (*Amwal*, 405, no 940). Probably, somebody somewhere had the text of a letter from the Prophet and speculatively constructed this history. Other reports are only slightly more credible; for example, 'Ali is quoted as urging people, "Who will buy religious knowledge from me for a dirham?" Abu Khaythamah, one of our ninth-century sources, interprets this as meaning who would buy, for a dirham each, sheets on which to write religious knowledge (meaning hadith; *'Ilm*, 34–5; *'Ilal* 1:213 *1:96*). One can hardly believe that this busy warrior and politician should have anticipated the interests and technical terminology of the hadith transmitters of two centuries later. Another Companion of the Prophet, Ibn 'Abbas, is quoted as asking "Who will buy religious knowledge from me for a dirham?" (*'Ilal* 1:213 1:96). It seems likely that the phrase was speculatively projected back onto various early figures.

Harder still to explain, for those who insist that hadith were normally transmitted in writing, are contradictory quotations for and against writing hadith from the same persons. For example, Sha'bi, whom I quoted earlier speaking against relating information from notes, is also quoted as urging, "When you hear something, write it down, even on the wall" while denying that he had ever resorted to written notes: "I have never written black on white" (*'Ilal* 1:216 1:97; *Hilyah* 4:321). It is axiomatic that, where there are contradictory reports about the past, the report that agrees with later orthodoxy will be the less reliable. When people make up descriptions of the past, consciously or otherwise, their inventions will agree with the present, not make the past seem more different. Renaissance paintings show the Roman soldiers who crucified Christ wearing Renaissance armor. It's easy to tell when a historical film was made: look at the leading actress's hairstyle. Given a report that a prominent early jurisprudent opposed writing down any revelation but the Qur'an, and another that the same man favored writing down what the Prophet had said, the most natural interpretation is that opposition to writing preceded its acceptance, and so the report favoring writing is simply a projection from the time when writing was becoming acceptable. Moreover, it seems unlikely that opposition to writing should have grown up in the eighth century if writing had been normal in the seventh.

Modern scholars who think that early acceptance of writing guarantees the reliability of the hadith are arguing in exactly the opposite way from medieval Muslims. For them, face-to-face communication ensured accuracy, not written notes. Khalaf ibn Tamim (died 206/821–2) is said to have heard ten thousand hadith from the great Kufan shaykh Sufyan al-Thawri (died 161/777?) but discarded his notebooks because he had not memorized the hadith they contained (*Muhaddith*, 601). Early Arabic script was fairly crude, often missing diacritical marks and almost always missing signs for short vowels. Early note-taking necessarily depended on some degree of memorization to work at all. Moreover, to people for whom writing was fairly new, there may have been a richness to recalling somebody's voice conspicuously lacking from the bare record of words on papyrus.

In one sense, medieval Muslims were right to prefer oral transmission. In our culture of written transmission, accuracy means reproducing what others have said, in exactly their words. During the ninth century, a similar standard took hold among Muslim scholars. We can compare quotations from al-Dhahabi (died 748/1348?) with the text of the biographical dictionary of Ibn Sa'd (died 230/845) and see something very close to word-for-word accuracy. However, when we compare texts from within the ninth century, such as quotations from al-Shafi'i and books supposedly written by him, it is clear that compilers felt free to present as quotation not the very words that someone had said but actually more the gist of what he had said, or even what they were sure he would have said had he still been around to say it. There is even more variation in the way ninth-century writers quoted eighth-century thinkers.

The medieval Sunni tradition does not say that we may depend on knowing the very words of the Prophet. Because all we have of the Prophet's teaching is the gist, medieval philologists repeatedly quote the Qur'an to illustrate good Arabic usage but seldom quote hadith. Muslim scholars could see there was too much paraphrasing for that to be safe. Ahmad quotes Sufyan al-Thawri as saying, "If I told you I've been relating hadith to you just as I've heard, I'd be lying" (*'Ilal* 1:550 *1:201*). Asked to relate hadith verbatim, Sufyan said, "No, by

God – there is no way to do so. It is only meanings" (*Hilyah* 6:370). That is, it was impossible to remember another's precise words. The accuracy these scholars aimed at was mainly, it seems, closeness to orthodoxy. Oral transmission assured closeness to orthodoxy, as teachers kept watch over students and students could not challenge current common knowledge by pointing to texts that contradicted it.

Ahmad was willing to paraphrase hadith. For example, the *Musnad* includes these two hadith reports:

> Waki' < Hisham < his father < 'A'ishah, 'The Prophet used to lower his head to me while he was *mujawir*, meaning *mu'takif* [living in withdrawal in the mosque], while I was in my chamber. I would wash and comb it even though I was menstruating'.

> (*Musnad* 6:204 *42:455*)

> Waki' < Hisham ibn 'Urwah < his father < 'A'ishah that she used to comb the Prophet's hair even though she was menstruating.

> (*Musnad* 6:208 *42:480*)

The first example directly quotes 'A'ishah, the Prophet's youngest and favorite wife; the second is presumably Ahmad's formulation of the essential point of law that 'A'ishah's statement establishes. However, the first includes a gloss on the term *mujawir* that seems odd coming from 'A'ishah and is much more likely to be a later transmitter's interpolation. Furthermore, one or more of the transmitters of the quotation might actually have remembered the point, such as Ahmad states it later, then reconstructed the words he believed 'A'ishah would have used. We do not know, and the tradition does not tell us we know, that there was a continuous memory of 'A'ishah's very words.

Ahmad himself strongly advocated written notes as an aid to memory. He forbade his son 'Abd Allah and his contemporary 'Ali ibn al-Madini (died 234/849) to relate hadith without their notebooks to hand. He himself almost never related hadith without his notebook (*TMD* 5:279–80). He said that the Meccan, Ibn Jurayj, had been more reliable when he related hadith from his notebooks than when he related from memory, as had others (*TB* 10:405), and that the Basran, Hammam ibn Yahya (died 164/780–1?), was much more reliable toward the end of his life, as his declining powers forced him to dictate from his notebook, and so he seldom made mistakes (*'Ilal* 1:357 *1:141*).

Ahmad was even a moderate advocate of transmitting the hadith entirely by writing. Yahya ibn Adam (died 203/818–19) was a Kufan traditionist. "He would bring out his notebooks to us," Ahmad recalled, "so we would write without listening" (*Siyar* 11:190). In other words, they copied his notebooks directly, without the usual corroboration of dictation. One of his closest disciples quoted him: "If I give you my notebook and tell you, "Relate this from me" and it is my hadith, what do you care whether you heard it or not?" (IAY, 1:57). Unlike Khalaf ibn Tamim, Ahmad thought it was acceptable to use someone's notebook to relate hadith that he did not actually remember, provided that he recognized the notebook as his (*Sirah*, 34). Nevertheless, in the major collections of Ahmad's hadith, the *Musnad* and the *Zuhd*, his son 'Abd Allah distinguishes between hadith he heard from his father and hadith he merely found in his notebooks. In making the distinction, he acknowledged the prevailing ethic that purely written transmission was second-rate compared with a combination of dictation and writing.

After Isma'il ibn 'Ulayyah, there is little further opposition to writing hadith. Ahmad's younger contemporary, Abu Zur'ah al-Razi (died 264/878), compared hadith with the Qur'an:

"When I become ill for a month or two, it noticeably affects my memory of the Qur'an. As for hadith, you will notice the effect if you leave it for (a few) days" (*Siyar* 13:79). That is, Abu Zur'ah continually returned his notebooks to refresh his memory of the hadith, whereas he needed to go through the whole Qur'an only once a month to remember it. I imagine this is the experience of most people who have committed anything to memory: unless we periodically return to the printed version, we forget. (The other common technique for keeping hadith reports fresh in the memory was *mudhakarah,* a memory contest, in which one traditionist would relate a hadith report with full *isnad*, another would mention a corroborating *isnad*, someone would mention a third and so on.)

Contrary to the opinion of early Muslims, in practice written notes increased the reliability of the hadith, as least in terms of their textual stability. From the tenth century onwards, there are increasing numbers of stories of frauds detected by inspection of notebooks. Abu Hafs 'Umar ibn Sa'id al-Dimashqi was relating hadith from the Syrian Sa'id ibn Bashir (died 169/785–6?). However, when Ahmad and Abu Khaythamah checked his notebook, they found the hadith was actually from the Basran, Sa'id ibn Abi 'Arubah (died 157/773–4?), evidently not so rare (*'Ilal* 3:210–11 *2:161*). Original notebooks sometimes confirmed someone's claim; for example, the Baghdadi, Ahmad ibn al-Hasan al-Sufi (died 306/919), was accused of forging hadith but vindicated himself by producing his ancient notebook (*asl*; *TB* 4:83).

So, from the tenth and eleventh centuries, the ubiquity of notebooks evidently made traditionists feel comfortable with the thought of hadith being passed on to five-year-olds: the written records would be reliable even if they could not be sure that the children could keep in their memories exactly what they had heard, with all its legal implications. From this point, traditionists no longer valued face-to-face oral transmission for its superior reliability but for the way it guaranteed their control over their material. They also valued the way it reproduced the experience of the Companions gathered around the Prophet, or at least connected them, by a chain of face-to-face encounters, with the Prophet himself.

AHMAD'S QUEST FOR HADITH

One of the first people from whom Ahmad heard hadith (but perhaps mainly other learning, namely law) was the qadi Abu Yusuf (died 182/798?), the famous disciple of the controversial jurisprudent Abu Hanifah (*Manaqib*, 22–3 26; Ibn Kathir, 10:181, 326). Ahmad remembered that he spoke with a lisp and defended him as a major exemplar of hadith (Ibn Hani', 2:235). However, when he started out in Baghdad, his principal teacher was Hushaym ibn Bashir, who dictated his hadith in categories. He later reminisced:

> We wrote from him the book of pilgrimage, about a thousand hadith reports, some of qur'anic commentary, the book of judgeship and some short books. They were [altogether] about three thousand.

> (*Sirah*, 34)

Ahmad also sometimes related hadith by category.

Famous hadith transmitters did come to Baghdad. Ahmad heard the Khurasani, Qutaybah ibn Sa'id (died 240/854–5), a major source for Bukhari and Muslim, in both Mecca and Baghdad (*Jarh* 1:299, 7:140). However, Ahmad travelled to get most of his material. When Hushaym died, Ahmad made his first trip out of Baghdad, to Kufa, in the same year, AH 183. With an Arab comrade, he walked there, more than 140 kilometers, barefoot.

In Kufa, he slept with a mud brick for a pillow; another report says that he slept with a mud brick on the floor, then a sack containing his notebooks on the brick, then his head on the sack (*Sirah*, 31, 33; *Siyar* 11:186). In 186/802, he made his first trip to Basra. A year after that, he made the first of five pilgrimages to Mecca (*Sirah*, 32).

The spreading of hadith was a pious enterprise. If they had sufficient means, great teachers would personally support bright students who wished to learn but Ahmad was noted for refusing aid. Yahya ibn Ma'in (died 233/848), who became an almost equally renowned hadith critic, accepted five hundred dirhams from the famous shaykh of Wasit (in Iraq), Yazid ibn Harun (died 206/821–2). Ahmad accepted nothing (*Hilyah* 9:177). 'Abd al-Razzaq (died 211/827) said that while Ahmad was studying under him (he stayed there almost two years), he offered him a purse full of gold coins but Ahmad refused, insisting that he was well (*Hilyah* 9:174–5). During his study under Sufyan ibn 'Uyaynah in Mecca, Ahmad failed to appear for several days. When his friends searched him out, they found his clothes had been stolen and so he could not go out in public. He was offered loans and gifts but refused them. He was finally prevailed on to earn a little money copying some notebooks and so was able to replace his stolen clothing (*TMD* 5:249). He once financed a journey between Mecca and Yemen by hiring himself out to some camel herders (*Jarh* 1:301). In Yemen, one of his occupations was weaving trouser strings (*tikak*; *Siyar* 11:193). Walking to Tarsus, he gathered fallen fruit (*Manaqib*, 225 308).

One alternative to being supported by one's teachers was private wealth. Ahmad did what he could to finance his own travels; for example, by selling his pearl earrings. Some students did better with their family resources. There are several reports of students who sold goods to pay for their travels,

such as Abu Zur'ah al-Razi, who decided to stay longer in
Egypt than he had planned and sold two garments to pay for it
(*Jarh* 1:340). Ishaq ibn Rahawayh was able to buy a concubine
in each new city. In Yemen, he proposed to exchange rooms
with Ahmad, who was on the floor below them and possibly
bothered by their noise. Ahmad would not put them to the
trouble (*TMD* 5:304).

It was a pious act for the rich, if they did not collect and
transmit hadith themselves, to give alms to "the people of the
mosque," meaning especially those whose life's work this was.
Al-Shafi'i took money from traders and land owners, among
others (Shirazi, 151). A trader once sent Ahmad four thousand dirhams, the profit of a trade with Samarqand, but after
a night of prayer, Ahmad sent it back (*Manaqib*, 229 *312–13*).
Stories are often told of the bounty of the caliph al-Ma'mun
(reigned 198–218/813–33) to traditionists. Once, he gave out
money through an intermediary, Ishaq ibn Musa al-Ansari: all
who were offered anything accepted save Ahmad ibn Hanbal
(*Hilyah* 9:181).

His objection to accepting anything was partly, no doubt, his
pride in being self-sufficient. A prophetic hadith report (with
half a dozen occurrences in the *Musnad*) advises, "Ask nothing
of [other] people, even your whip if it falls [from your hand]."
Self-sufficiency might guard against the temptation to compro-
mise one's religion. Yahya ibn Ma'in caved in at the Inquisition
and professed, as the caliph demanded, that the Qur'an was
created. Perhaps Ahmad resisted because he habitually said
"no." Certain customs developed that protected needy men of
religion from temptation; for example, it was normal to accept
a gift before giving a juridical opinion (*fatwa*) rather than after,
since the giver could not then withhold his gift if presented
with an unfavorable opinion. However, these customs could
look dubious. The great Basran hadith collector Abu Dawud al-

Tayalisi (died 204/819?) came to Isfahan in the 160s/777–87 and gave *tayalisah* (ceremonial scarves) to notables, for which each would give him one thousand dirhams. He refused other gifts. When he left, after some months, he had thirty thousand dirhams (Abu al-Shaykh, 2:50).

In 197/812–13, Ahmad was again living in Mecca. He and his companion, Yahya ibn Ma'in, had resolved to make the pilgrimage, then travel on to Yemen to hear hadith from 'Abd al-Razzaq. Yahya ibn Ma'in spotted 'Abd al-Razzaq in Mecca, at the Ka'bah, and proposed that they hear his dictation there. Ahmad refused, saying he would not contravene his *niyah*, the express intention he had made when undertaking the pilgrimage (*TMD* 5:266–7). During the year 199/814–15, they lived in the house of 'Abd al-Razzaq, in the Sanaa region.

This mention of 'Abd al-Razzaq's house brings up the subject of where people went to hear hadith. In the early days, the mosque was the site of all Islamic administration; for example, judges normally sat in mosques. Naturally, mosques were also the sites of preaching, both formal and informal, and of religious instruction, and hence the transmission of hadith. We probably have more references to the transmission of hadith in mosques than anywhere else. Ahmad first related hadith (as opposed to collecting it) and offered juridical opinions in a mosque near Mecca (*Manaqib*, 187–8 256). Within the mosque, listeners sat on the ground in circles. "He sat with Qatadah" was equivalent to saying "He heard hadith from Qatadah." They avoided sitting in dirt but dry earth was presumed clean, so that they did not need to sweep it before praying, let alone before sitting there. However, by the ninth century, there are frequent references to mats, considered a reprehensible innovation just a century before. Once, attending a funeral, Ahmad refused to sit on a mat borrowed from the local mosque (and hence public property wrongly appropriated for private use): instead, he sat on the bare earth (*Wara'*, 31 32).

The leader of the circle would commonly sit with his back to a pillar. To sit against a pillar was so strongly identified with teaching that Ahmad's teacher, Sufyan ibn 'Uyaynah, referred to the first person to ask him to relate hadith as "the first to make me lean against the pillar" (*TB* 9:176). Shoes were removed, and laid to one's left. It was good manners to sit wherever there happened to be a space but the place of honor was that nearest the leader of the circle; there are many stories of students who impressed the teacher by their knowledge and were asked to come closer. Etiquette prescribed that students sit with their knees drawn up and their hands (or a special belt) clasped around them, or with their legs folded. Leaning back on the hand was frowned on.

After the mosque, teaching is next most frequently mentioned as happening in the teacher's own home. Ahmad recollected, "We heard of the death of Hammad ibn Zayd when we were at Hushaym's door, as Hushaym was dictating to us [hadith] concerning funerals" (*TMD* 5:264). Ahmad once listened to hadith from Waki' at the gate of his house until far into the night, when a slave girl came out to remind them how late it was (presumably to get Waki' to bed, he being in his seventies at the time; *TI* 18:68). He initially accosted 'Abd al-Razzaq outside his house (*Manaqib*, 152 204–5).

A traditionist might prefer to dictate in his house because that is where his notes were. There is a story of Ahmad dictating hadith at the mosque, when someone asked him about a particular hadith report. He asked his son 'Abd Allah to pass him a particular notebook but it turned out not to be there, so Ahmad went to his house and came back with a stack of notebooks, through which he went, one after another, looking for the report in question (*Manaqib*, 189–90 259). It would have been easier had the students been at his house to begin with. The house also presented advantages over the mosque if the teacher wanted to offer hospitality to the listeners, as did several of Ahmad's shaykhs. The Kufan, Hafs ibn Ghiyath (died 194/810?), declared, "Whoever has not eaten of our food, we will not relate hadith to him" (*TB* 8:194). It was also advantageous for less reputable teachers who demanded payment for their hadith, such as the Baghdadi, Ibn Abi Usamah al-Tamimi (died 282/896). A traditionist related finding a crowd of booksellers in his vestibule, whose names Ibn Abi Usamah was writing down: each was to pay him two dirhams (*Lisan* 2:157–8). (Ahmad firmly opposed hearing hadith from anyone who demanded payment, "even for politeness's sake" [IAY, 1:169].) Finally, it was easier to withdraw from a session at home, as Ahmad did when a student related to the group that somebody in Mecca had disparaged the traditionists: at this Ahmad rose, shook his clothes, spoke the word *zindiq* (secret unbeliever) three times and retired into his house (*Manaqib*, 179–80 247).

For some twenty-five years, Ahmad collected hadith. He travelled throughout Iraq, to Tarsus on the Byzantine frontier, and to Arabia. He did not travel to some important centers. The lack of fifty dirhams, he lamented, meant he never went to hear from Jarir (died 188/803–4), a Kufan who had settled in Ray, near present-day Tehran (*Sirah*, 32–3). He also declared that lack of money had prevented him from going to Khurasan (present-day north-eastern Iran and western Afghanistan) to hear from Yahya ibn Yahya (died 224/839?), a major source of hadith for Bukhari and Muslim (*Manaqib*, 29 34). He never went to Egypt and, more surprisingly, it is doubtful he ever travelled to Medina, about 350 kilometers north of Mecca. Some 34 percent of the hadith reports in the *Musnad* are from Baghdadi shaykhs, 28 from Basran and 15 from Kufan. Altogether, the *Musnad* is about 86 percent Iraqi. Yemeni shaykhs (mostly 'Abd al-Razzaq) account for almost 6 percent, Meccan for almost 5, and Syrian for almost 4 but there are scarcely two dozen reports from Medinan shaykhs – fewer than one in a thousand. All the biographies assert that Ahmad's travels included Medina but it seems more likely that he heard from the Medinans when they themselves were travelling, most likely in Mecca or Basra.

THE *MUSNAD*

Asked how long he would keep on going with "these boys" in quest of hadith, Ahmad answered, "till death" (*TB* 6:274). Indeed, the *Musnad* includes hadith reports from a few shaykhs who were still alive when Ahmad died. He seems to have stopped travelling, settled down and concentrated on sorting and selecting his hadith in about 205/820–1, when he was forty or so and first married. This is when he began to relate hadith to others and also, it is said, when he began work on the *Musnad*. He did make one more important trip from Baghdad, travelling to Syria when his son Salih was about six years old (*Siyar* 11:306).

Ahmad seems to have experimented early on with arranging hadith by topic. Abu Hatim al-Razi (d. 277/890–1) recalled:

> I first met Ahmad in the year 213 [828–9]. He had brought out with him to the prayer the book of drinks and the book of faith. He then prayed. Nobody asked him anything, so he returned his books to his house. I came to him another day. Lo and behold, he had brought out the same two books. I thought he was doing so to fulfil his duty of upholding public morals, for the book of faith is the root of the faith, while the book of drinks

means turning people away from evil, all evil coming from drunkenness.

(*Jarh* 1:303)

Ahmad clearly brought, probably at the dawn prayer, two topical collections of hadith to the mosque – and stubbornly kept on bringing them even though no one seemed to be interested.

Various authorities of the eighth century are credited with being the first to arrange hadith topically: in Basra, al-Rabi' ibn Sabih (died 160/776–7) and in Kufa, Sufyan al-Thawri or Ibn Abi Za'idah (died 183/799?; *Muhaddith*, 611–12, *Jarh* 9:144). In the 1990s, Miklos Muranyi uncovered and published a page from what appears to be a topical collection by 'Abd al-'Aziz ibn al-Majishun (died 164/780–1), a Medinan jurisprudent who went to Baghdad late in life; however, we cannot be certain whether it was Ibn al-Majishun himself who did the arranging or a later scholar. We are also told of a version of Malik's *Muwatta'*, a topically arranged collection of hadith and opinions, that was introduced to North Africa in 150/767–8 (*Muw*. 'Ali). There was initially some opposition to the new style. Ibn al-Mubarak was reproached by Abu Usamah (possibly Hammad ibn Usamah, a Kufan, died 201/816–17) for classifying and sorting hadith in a way previous shaykhs had not done. Penitent, Ibn al-Mubarak resolved to avoid hadith for twenty days but relapsed because of his self-acknowledged "lust for hadith" (*Hilyah* 8:165). (There is more in chapter five on tension between traditionists and renunciants.) However, arrangement by topic was well established by the time Ahmad began to sort his hadith. Arrangement by Companion seems to have come later than by topic. The first person in Basra to arrange hadith this way was said to have been Ahmad's shaykh, Abu Dawud al-Tayalisi; in Kufa, 'Ubayd Allah ibn Musa (died 213/829?; Khalili, 149?).

Eventually, Ahmad chose arrangement by transmitter. The *Musnad* is Ahmad's principal collection of hadith (or any other teaching). The name, meaning "supported," refers first to the way every hadith report in it has an *isnad*, a chain of authority going back to the original speaker. Some important collections of hadith from Ahmad's lifetime include much material from later Muslims. In 'Abd al-Razzaq's *Musannaf* and the *Musannaf* of Ahmad's Kufan contemporary, Ibn Abi Shaybah (died 235/849), scarcely one report in five goes back to the Prophet: the rest are the opinions of Companions, Followers and other eighth-century jurisprudents. There is also an extant, smaller collection of hadith from Ibn Abi Shaybah, also called the *Musnad*, which is entirely prophetic; Ahmad's *Musnad* is overwhelmingly prophetic. The only major exception is near the beginning, in the sections devoted to hadith from *al-khulafa' al-rashidun*, (the Rightly-Guided Caliphs). Ahmad defined the authoritative *sunnah*, the normative precedent, as that laid down by the Prophet and these four caliphs. Hence, for example, there are items like this:

> < 'Attab ibn Ziyad < 'Abd Allah, that is, Ibn al-Mubarak < Yunus < al-Zuhri < al-Sa'ib ibn Yazid and 'Ubayd Allah ibn 'Abd Allah ibn 'Utbah < 'Abd al-Rahman ibn 'Abd < 'Umar: Whoever omits something of his *wird* or *hizb* in the night, let him recite it between the dawn prayer and the noon. It will be as if he had recited it at night.
>
> (*Musnad* 1:32 1:343–4)

This refers to a supererogatory prayer, a private liturgy, or a section of the Qur'an to be recited at a special night vigil (early usage was insufficiently strict for us to say for sure which one). The Six Books (the principal Sunni collections of hadith) also include a few hadith reports going back to leading Companions.

Ahmad's *Musnad* is principally arranged not by shaykh but by Companion; that is, the person who first reported something the Prophet had said or done. *Musnad* is sometimes used to designate a collection arranged by *isnad*, as opposed to a *musannaf* arranged by topic (*sinf*). Ahmad assembled the *Musnad* mainly from notebooks of hadith he had heard from various shaykhs. At his death, it was estimated that his library came to twelve and a half camel loads (*Manaqib*, 60 74–5). Abu Zur'ah al-Razi found it notable that he had not written on the first or last page of each notebook the name of the shaykh from whom these hadith reports had come, which was the usual practice; rather, he recognized from whom he had heard each set of hadith reports by the reports themselves (*Jarh* 1:296). There is a vestige of Ahmad's original notes in the common occurrence of series of hadith reports from the same shaykh; for example, a series of reports with Waki' < someone at one end and Ibn 'Abbas < the Prophet at the other.

The advantage of arrangement by topic is making it much easier to look up a given hadith report. This is probably one reason the most popular Sunni collections of hadith, the Six Books, are all arranged by topic. Ahmad's *Musnad* did not become so popular – indeed was almost lost – in part because it was inconveniently arranged. (It must be making a comeback now on easily-searchable electronic versions.) Arrangement by Companion reflects the habit of traditionists, who thought first of *isnad*, although jurisprudents habitually referred to different hadith reports by Companion; for example, "We go by Ibn 'Umar's hadith report, whereas the Hanafiyah rely on 'A'ishah's." Perhaps half consciously, Ahmad and his son 'Abd Allah, to whom he dictated the *Musnad* and in whose name it was published, preferred a difficult arrangement just to make the point that one had to be a competent traditionist to handle Islamic law. Topical arrangement would let in too many dilettantes, who did not know which hadith reports were well attested and therefore risked relying on spurious ones.

Another reason for the relative neglect of Ahmad's *Musnad* is its inconvenient bulk. Medieval estimates of its extent range from thirty to forty thousand hadith. Modern printed versions and extant manuscripts contain about 27,600. This compares with the approximately 7,400 hadith reports in Bukhari's *Sahih*, the most highly reputed of the Six Books. The first modern edition of the *Musnad*, printed in Cairo in the 1890s, comprises six volumes, some 3,000 pages, of small print. The most recent, and best, printed version, edited by Shu'ayb al-Arna'ut and others in Syria and Lebanon, takes up fifty volumes. Before modern printing, when books had to be copied by hand, it was rare to come across a complete copy of the *Musnad*. Most scholars had only fragments. A Syrian Hanbali scholar of the early twentieth century reported that many of his shaykhs maintained that the *Musnad* was altogether lost (*Madkhal*, 471). To some extent, estimates of its length varied because of differences among manuscripts. Copyists seem to have been especially inclined to omit additional hadith from 'Abd Allah that he had not heard from his father. However, it is evident from medieval quotations that some manuscripts included numbers of hadith reports from Ahmad no longer found in modern versions (for example, numbers one and two in the sequence of seven sample hadith below).

The *Musnad* is much longer than the Six Books largely because of repetitions. The *Sahih* of Bukhari comprises about 7,400 hadith reports but somewhat fewer than 2,800 distinct reports; there are approximately two repeats for each *matn*. In contrast, the extant text of the *Musnad* comprises about 27,600 reports but only some 5,200 different reports: a ratio of four repeats to one original.

In both Bukhari's and Ahmad's collections, some repeats are exact duplications but most give the same text with different *isnad*s. For example, the Prophet's saying, "If only you knew what I know, you would laugh little and weep much" is quoted six times under five different headings in Bukhari's *Sahih*: it ends a long speech made on the occasion of an eclipse, hence it appears in the chapter on eclipses (from 'A'ishah); shorn of any mention of an eclipse, it appears with the same *isnad* in the chapter on marriages; with a somewhat different *isnad* and a small addition ("By God"), it appears in the chapter on oaths; with a completely different *isnad* (from Anas ibn Malik), it appears in the chapter on explaining the Qur'an, where it is followed by an account of the Companions' strong reaction; and, finally, the chapter on *riqaq* (sayings to soften the heart) includes these two short versions, one after another:

> 1 < Yahya ibn Bukayr < al-Layth < 'Uqayl < Ibn Shihab < Sa'id ibn al-Musayyab < Abu Hurayrah < the Messenger of God: If only you knew what I know, you would laugh little and weep much.

> 2 < Sulayman ibn Harb < Shu'bah < Musa ibn Anas < Anas < the Prophet: If only you knew what I know, you would laugh little and weep much.

The *isnad* of the second version resembles the *isnad* of the version in the chapter on the Qur'an.

The *Musnad* includes twenty-three versions of this saying. One is identical in *isnad* and almost in *matn* to the version Bukhari has in the chapter on eclipses (the difference in *matn* is to do with repeated phrases and probably goes back to copying errors made well after Ahmad's time). Three are close parallels to Bukhari's first version ("Ibn Shihab" and "al-Zuhri" are the same person):

1 'Abd Allah < his father < Sufyan < al-Zuhrî < Sa'id ibn al-Musayyab < Abu Hurayrah < the Messenger of God: If only you knew what I know, you would laugh little and weep much.

(*Itraf* 7:274)

2 'Abd Allah < his father < 'Abd al-Razzaq < Ma'mar < al-Zuhri < Sa'id ibn al-Musayyab < Abu Hurayrah < the Messenger of God: If only you knew what I know, you would laugh little and weep much.

(*Itraf* 7:274)

3 'Abd Allah < his father < Hajjaj < Layth < 'Uqayl < Ibn Shihab < Sa'id ibn al-Musayyab < Abu Hurayrah < the Messenger of God: If only you knew what I know, you would laugh little and weep much.

(*Musnad* 2:453 *15:527*)

The *Musnad* thus gives three paths of transmission branching out from Zuhri, while Bukhari's *Sahih* has a fourth. The *Musnad* has four parallels to the second version from Bukhari:

4 'Abd Allah < his father < Sulayman and Abu Sa'id, that is, the client to Bani Hashim < Shu'bah < Musa ibn Anas < Anas < the Prophet: If only you knew what I know, you would laugh little and weep much.

(*Musnad* 3:210 *20:417–18*)

5 'Abd Allah < his father < 'Affan < Shu'bah < Musa ibn Anas < Anas < the Prophet: If only you knew what I know, you would laugh little and weep much.

(*Musnad* 3:268 *21:333*)

6 'Abd Allah < his father < Muhammad ibn Fudayl < al-Mukhtar ibn Fulful < Anas ibn Malik < the Messenger of God

one day, when he had left the prayer and approached us: "O people, I am your prayer leader, so do not go ahead of us in either inclination or prostration, in either standing or sitting, or in leaving. I see you behind me and before me. By him in whose hand is my soul, if you had seen what I have seen, you would laugh little and weep much". They said, "O Messenger of God, what have you seen?" He said, "I have seen Paradise and Hell".

(*Musnad* 3:102 *19:56–8*)

< 'Abd Allah < his father < 'Abd al-Samad ibn 'Abd al-Warith < Za'idah < al-Mukhtar ibn Fulful < Anas ibn Malik < the Messenger of God: "By him in whose hand is Muhammad's soul, if you had seen what I have seen, you would laugh little and weep much". They said, "O Messenger of God, what have you seen?" He said, "I have seen Paradise and Hell".

(*Musnad* 3:126 *19:294–5*)

The point is clear: the discouragement of laughing and the encouragement of weeping, a favorite devotional practice of eighth-century Muslim renunciants. Weeping is still commonly seen at Shi'i pilgrimage sites and at, to a lesser extent, the recitation of the Qur'an. The names were as tedious for medieval non-specialists to read as they are for present-day ones, which is why books aimed at a general audience usually omit them. For example, they are omitted from *Riyad al-salihin* (The gardens of the pious) by al-Nawawi (died 676/1277). A prominent Syrian mufti described this collection to me as the single best collection of hadith for a pious Muslim family to keep in the house, for it is so full of good advice. Nawawi was a great hadith authority and expected his readers to trust that he had not made up his material.

What do the names tell us? Some modern Muslims argue that the Companions and later traditionists were too good at memorizing (we have only to consider the amount of poetry they transmitted verbatim) and too careful not to distort what they had heard from the Seal of the Prophets to have changed a word. The last two hadith reports above would have to have come from the Prophet on two different occasions, as would Bukhari's two versions with and without an oath. This is not what the medieval tradition maintained. In the face of so much contrary evidence, it seems to have only polemical convenience to recommend it.

Other scholars, inclined to take the names seriously and to allow a little more slippage in transmission, look at number two from Bukhari and numbers four to seven from Ahmad and point to al-Mukhtar ibn Fulful as the person who must have changed the wording; for example replacing "if only you knew" with "if you had seen." But then how do we explain the attachment of this saying to the warning about praying properly, since the Prophet can see behind him as well as before? This warning crops up in numerous other hadith reports (for example, Muslim offers four in a row under the heading of "praying well"), with no mention of laughing and weeping. The drift of phrases in and out of different hadith reports is a fairly common phenomenon. Marston Speight has studied various readings in different hadith collections and concludes that they reflect oral performance, especially the concern "to clothe the prophetic dicta in effective rhetorical dress to enhance their religious significance" (Speight, 175). In the traditionists' view, it was a good thought, they were sure the Prophet had said it, and it made little practical difference precisely in which context or wording it was quoted. Whatever the explanation of differences, the major point is that Bukhari to some extent and Ahmad to a much greater do not ask us to take their word for what the Prophet said but present the evidence, mainly the *isnads*, for us to examine for ourselves.

The *Musnad* contains far less than the sum of Ahmad's knowledge, even of hadith. Abu Zur'ah al-Razi told 'Abd Allah that he thought his father had known a million, basing his estimate on the memory contests he had enjoyed with Ahmad (*TMD* 5:246). This number includes many hadith reports from later figures than the Prophet but must also include many more prophetic hadith than found their way into the *Musnad*. Ahmad's recollection has already been mentioned that he heard about 3,000 hadith reports from Hushaym; yet the *Musnad* includes fewer than 300 from him. Ibn al-Jawzi names 414 men and one woman from whom Ahmad learnt hadith, whereas the *Musnad* comprises hadith from only 292 shaykhs, some 70 percent of the total (*Manaqib*, bab 5; *Mu'jam*, 9). Many hadith reports from the Prophet not in the *Musnad* are found in Ahmad's collection *al-Zuhd*.

Some readers will be particularly interested to hear about female traditionists. As the list of Ahmad's authorities shows, they existed but only in very small numbers. When we imagine Ahmad walking from city to city, sitting in a circle at the mosque or copying hadith at the door of a shaykh's house, it is easy to see what the principal hindrance to female expertise in hadith was: well-bred women did not sit in public places or travel alone. Only in the later Middle Ages did women become a significant proportion of active traditionists. My guess is that this came about because by then the point of knowing great quantities of hadith was no longer to be able to form correct opinions about the revealed law, as it was for Ahmad, but to mark one's membership of the upper class.

HADITH CRITICISM

"It was the principal work of Ahmad's life to collect and sort hadith." Sorting not only meant arranging hadith by topic or transmitter but also deciding which reports were reliable and which not. Some Muslims of Ahmad's time thought that practically no hadith reports were sufficiently well attested to rely on. This was notably the position of certain Mu'tazilah, who asserted that they would follow only such hadith as were reported by twelve, twenty, or seventy witnesses in each generation (the numbers come from various stories in the Qur'an).

In books about the theory of Islamic law, Mu'tazili writers used the term *mutawatir*, meaning "so widely transmitted that no one could doubt it." The Qur'an was *mutawatir*: so many Muslims had passed on the text of the Qur'an to so many others that there could be no possibility of fraud. A hypothetical objection to this standard was that the New Testament had also been passed on from innumerable Christians to innumerable others, yet was manifestly fraudulent; for example, it asserted that Jesus was killed, then raised again from the dead, whereas the Qur'an clearly indicates that the Jews failed to crucify him (which would have been an insupportable affront to one of God's prophets). The answer was that whereas the New Testament might have been *mutawatir* for a long time, it was not at the very start. The four Evangelists might have conspired to perpetrate a fraud – indeed, plainly had. Practically none of the Sunni party's beloved hadith reports were *mutawatir* in the way the Qur'an was.

Other Muslims cited hadith when arguing with those who disagreed with them on points of law but for the most part expounded the law on the bases of common sense and local tradition. Their fashion of sorting contradictory hadith was crude. Some, like Malik and other defenders of the Medinan tradition, simply cited whatever supported their own positions and ignored whatever did not. Others, such as Shaybani, Abu

Hanifah's follower, would sometimes prefer whatever claimed to be older, such as hadith from Companions as opposed to hadith from Followers. Shafi'i quoted many hadith and often argued strenuously for following hadith from the Prophet rather than local tradition or expert opinion; however, when it comes to hadith with which he disagreed, he disqualified them by citing expert opinion, without analyzing them himself.

Ahmad's position was to stress the use of criticism to distinguish between reliable and unreliable hadith, and practiced it intensely himself. He was apparently one of the experts on whom Shafi'i relied, although without ever mentioning him by name. So far as I am aware, Ahmad never used the term *mutawatir* and on principle would not debate with the Mu'tazilah. It was presumably his view that even if most hadith reports were transmitted by four or fewer Companions (no more than the four Evangelists), all Companions were sufficiently virtuous not to have conspired to deceive. As for later transmitters, hadith criticism could demonstrate who was reliable.

No hadith critic was more highly renowned than Ahmad, except perhaps his contemporary, Yahya ibn Ma'in. When faced with contradictory hadith, Ahmad either used the critical method to dispose of one or, if neither would yield, simply refused to take a stand: he would not over rule hadith by appeals to reason or local custom, as other jurisprudents might do.

We have scant systematic descriptions of hadith criticism from the ninth century, so we must infer Ahmad's method from scattered examples. Very many of his evaluations are quoted in encyclopaedias of *rijal* criticism; that is, in the biographical dictionaries of traditionists. The earliest to quote Ahmad extensively is Bukhari's *al-Tarikh al-kabir*. This work is chiefly concerned with traditionists' names and only secondarily with from whom they transmitted and who transmitted from them but also offers an occasional evaluation. Most evaluations come from Bukhari himself, but Ahmad and a few other critics are also occasionally quoted, Ahmad more often than anyone else. Many quotations from Ahmad are found in *al-Jarh wa-al-ta'dil* by Ibn Abi Hatim al-Razi (died 327/938); for example:

> Ziyad ibn Abi Muslim [also said to be Ziyad ibn Muslim] was highly trustworthy, a pious man; "Abd Allah recalled that he had said of Ya'la ibn Hakim, 'trustworthy"; asked of Khalid ibn Ilyas al-Qurashi, he said, "abandoned in hadith", meaning that no one respectable related hadith of him.

> (*Jarh* 3:321, 547, 9:303).

Finding these simple characterizations next to facts about traditionists' lives (and perhaps influenced by descriptions of hadith criticism in books about the theory of Islamic law), modern scholars sometimes suppose that the basic method of hadith criticism was to examine a man's character and, on that basis, accept or reject his hadith. It is also alleged that hadith critics paid careful attention to when and where different traditionists were born, travelled and died, so that it could be known whether two people mentioned in an *isnad* could actually have met. However, examination of the earliest literature of hadith criticism makes both seem doubtful.

Too little is known of the characters of too many transmitters. The earliest biographical dictionaries from active hadith critics, such as Bukhari and Ibn Abi Hatim, say less about character than contemporary biographical dictionaries by littérateurs. Furthermore, it is unclear what characteristics disqualified people from transmitting hadith. The Basran, Shu'bah (died 160/776–7), was said to prefer 'Ali to 'Uthman (although not by Ahmad) but Ahmad accused him of being a Murji', with a flawed conception of faith and works (*Lisan* 3:433; *'Ilal* 2:145,

147 *1:249*). None the less, Shu'bah appears in almost a tenth of the *isnad*s in the *Musnad*. The Kufan, Jabir al-Ju'fi (died 127/744–5?), was alleged to be a *rafidi*, someone who rejected not only 'Uthman, but also Abu Bakr and 'Umar, in favor of 'Ali. Ahmad related that 'Abd al-Rahman ibn Mahdi and Yahya ibn Sa'id al-Qattan (two great Basran critics of the previous generation) refused to relate any of his hadith (*'Ilal* 1:503, 2:323, 3:158 *1:186, 311, 2:142*). Yet Ahmad is not known to have objected to his Shi'ism but rather to his making up hadith as a joke against Abu Hanifah ('Uqayli, 1:195–6). Even so, his name appears almost a hundred times in the *Musnad*. However, Ahmad struck out the hadith he had written down from the Baghdadi 'Ali ibn al-Ja'd (died 230/844–5) because he had disparaged some of the Companions (*TB* 11:365). There is no evidence of systematic inclusion or exclusion on theological grounds.

The earliest sources offer too few data on traditionists' precise birth and death dates for early authorities to have relied on them to sort hadith. The precise relationship of Bukhari's *rijal* encyclopedia, *al-Tarikh al-kabir*, to his chief collection of hadith, the *Sahih*, is unclear but al-Tarikh certainly does not provide enough dates for him to have used it to select on whom he could rely or not. Dates of death are given for only about 6 percent of its subjects and a date of birth for almost none. More death dates are found in later encyclopedias, but even Ibn Hajar (died 852/1449) mentions no date of death at all for about 60 percent of the transmitters in the Six Books, not even dates as approximate as "he died around (1)50." Multiple reports are very common; for example, Safwan ibn 'Isa al-Zuhri, one of Ahmad's Basran shaykhs, is recorded by Ibn Sa'd as having died in 200, by Bukhari in 198, by Ibn Hibban in 198 or the beginning of 199, and by another writer in Rajab 208 (*Tahdhib* 4:430). The simplest explanation is that such dates as we have for men of the seventh and eighth centuries are mostly inferences from who appears next to whom in *isnad*s (something to which the earliest encyclopedias do pay much attention) and not documentary evidence from birth certificates or baptismal records (unavailable in the Middle Ages) or the notes of traditionists who took dictation from them. Ahmad is even uncertain about which year Abu Yusuf died in (Ibn Hani', 2:168). Diaries seem to have become common from about the tenth century and it is only then that we may expect accurate dates of birth and death for prominent scholars. Famous as he was among traditionists, it is uncertain even in which month Ahmad died.

The best evidence for how ninth-century hadith critics worked is the critical literature of the ninth century. This confirms the descriptions of hadith criticism from the tenth century and strongly emphasizes the comparison of *isnad*s. Admittedly, unorthodox hadith were dismissed out of hand, without the usual tests. Could the Prophet really have said, "If you see Mu'awiyah on this pulpit, kill him" (*Sunnah*, 134 *151*)? Only a Shi'i might think so: to a Sunni like Ahmad, it was an article of faith that the Prophet's Companions were above criticism and no *isnad* could make such a *matn* credible. However, hadith criticism was usually much more difficult than that.

Our best source for Ahmad's practice is the collection *al-'Ilal wa-ma'rifat al-rijal* (Subtle defects and knowledge of men), assembled by his son 'Abd Allah. "Knowledge of men" refers first to establishing someone's identity, which takes up about a quarter of the *'Ilal* (and over 90 percent of *al-Tarikh al-kabir*); for example, "My father said, 'I more than once heard Isma'il ibn 'Ulayyah say, "There related to me Yahya, Abu Humam," meaning Abu Humam ibn Yahya'," thus identifying a man who appeared in *isnad*s from Ibn 'Ulayyah (*'Ilal* 2:542 *2:50*). "Knowledge of men" refers second to characterizing somebody's reliability as a transmitter of hadith, which takes up another quarter of the collection; for example, "Abu Zayd al-Harawi is trustworthy" ('*Ilal* 2:100 *1:236*).

How would Ahmad know that someone was trustworthy? His chief technique was to compare what he related from a given shaykh with what others related from him. If the shaykh's quotations were corroborated by others' he was probably reliable but if he continually related things no one else did, his reliability was questionable. For example, Ahmad says of Miskin ibn Bukayr, "He related hadith of Shu'bah that no one else did" (*Jarh* 8:329). This is usually a sign that something is wrong. Elsewhere he speaks more clearly: "I looked into the hadith reports that Miskin related of Shu'bah and there were errors among them" ('Uqayli, 4:221) and "He used to make mistakes concerning Shu'bah's hadith" (Ibn Hani', 2:203). Such a method makes sense: if character were what made traditionists trustworthy, not only was there too little information available to critics to make intelligent assessments but it would have been easy to make up *isnads* comprising only the names of the trustworthy.

Here is Ahmad detecting a mistake from one of his own shaykhs:

> The hadith report that Waki' related < Ibn Abi Dhi'b < Salih, client to the Taw'amah, < Ibn 'Abbas < the Prophet ... about combining the noon and afternoon prayers – this hadith report is actually Dawud ibn Qays's, not something Ibn Abi Dhi'b transmitted.

('*Ilal* 2:30 *1:216*)

Ahmad knew that Waki' alone related this hadith report from Ibn Abi Dhi'b, while everyone else related it from Dawud ibn Qays. Of course, Ahmad knew a great deal else from Waki' that was confirmed by other shaykhs, and the *Musnad* includes almost 1,900 hadith reports from him, presumably because the overwhelming majority of his quotations, unlike here, were corroborated by others.

The priority of comparing *isnad*s over characterizations of individuals' reliability is clear from examination of the *Musnad*. Ahmad is quoted as saying that Muhammad ibn Ishaq (died 151/768–9?), the famous biographer of the Prophet, was:

> a man from whom one may write such hadith reports as these, meaning stories of raids and the like. As for what he quotes concerning the licit and forbidden, we require strength like this whereupon he clenched his fist.

(*Jarh* 7:193)

Thus, one might expect the *Musnad* to include only historical reports from Ibn Ishaq. He appears in almost 600 *isnad*s, of which the first dozen are divided seven-to-five between rules (how to dress for the ritual prayer, how to perform the minor ritual ablution, how to divide the property of a man who has died in an accident) and history, roughly the same proportion as in the whole *Musnad*. What makes Ibn Ishaq worth quoting is that his transmission corroborates, and is corroborated by, parallel *isnad*s. Ahmad's method of hadith criticism is not to classify transmitters, then mechanically apply those classifications to all the hadith they transmit (like his modern editors, among others) but rather to accept as sound what is corroborated and reject as dubious what is not. Classifications, such as those of standard biographical dictionaries like Ibn Hajar's were meant to indicate where one needed corroboration, not whether to accept or reject any given hadith report.

A number of medieval critics tried to describe the criteria by which Bukhari and Muslim judged hadith reports sound

or not but it seems that none succeeded in covering all cases.
The *'Ilal* and similar collections of his hadith criticism suggest Ahmad used a case-by-case, seat-of-the-pants approach
to determining what was sound and what was not. The large
part played by intuition was sometimes acknowledged by the
medieval tradition itself. The Syrian jurisprudent, al-Awza'i
(died 157/774?), said:

> We used to hear hadith reports and offer them for inspection by
> our colleagues as one offers counterfeit dirhams for inspection.
> What they recognised, we took, what they rejected, we left.
>
> (*Muhaddith*, 318)

When someone challenged 'Abd al-Rahman ibn Mahdi, one
of Ahmad's leading Basran shaykhs, he retorted, "When you
go to an assayer with a dinar and he tells you it is counterfeit,
can you say to him 'Why do you say so?'" (*Muhaddith*, 312). He
preferred to rely on the feel he had developed over the years.
Of course, one critic's feel was bound to be different from
another's, hence the constant disagreement in collections of
hadith criticism. For example, different critics said of Miskin
ibn Bukayr (died 198/813–14), who appears in Bukhari's
and Muslim's famous collections, "not bad," "basically sound,"
"often imagined things and made mistakes," and "trustworthy"
(*Tahdhib* 10:121).

Ahmad reputedly thought that his *Musnad* said all that was
needed. His cousin, Hanbal ibn Ishaq (died 273/886), quoted
him as saying:

> I have collected and selected this book from 750,000.
> Whatever the Muslims disagree about by way of the hadith
> of the Messenger of God ... consult it. If you find it there ...
> otherwise, it is not probative.
>
> (IAY, 1:143)

In other words, in case of doubt, one should resort to the *Musnad*. If a disputed hadith report was found there, one might safely act on it; if it was not, one should disregard it. Actually, examination of other works reveals that Ahmad had his doubts about some of the hadith in the *Musnad* and respected some hadith not there. Hadith turned out to offer only a degree more certainty than other methods of arriving at God's will.

3

LAW

Ahmad's posthumous fame comes above all from his work as a jurisprudent. He strongly advocated relying on hadith, especially on prophetic hadith. In this way, his jurisprudence seems forward-looking, since this stress on textual sources (preponderantly on the hadith and also the Qur'an) came to prevail in the next millennium. In some ways, however, he looks more like the last of the old guard. His jurisprudence is pre-Classical: it gives more weight than later systems to hadith from others than the Prophet, it is often careless of the boundary between "required" and "recommended," and it still has traces of reliance on the speculation and practice of wise men. When his immediate followers recorded his opinions and even more when later adherents arranged them systematically and used them to construct an academic discipline, they took his teaching in a direction he would have found horrifying.

THE SPECTRUM OF OPINION IN THE NINTH CENTURY

It is unhistorical to say that Islam is essentially a religion of law: the Qur'an can be read in other ways, as above all an injunction to be loyal to the one true God (and his messenger) and as a warning of judgment to come. Many eighth-century Muslims demonstrably interpreted the Qur'an in this way (see chapter five). Some of Ahmad's contemporaries, mainly his Mu'tazili enemies, inclined towards an Islam in which theology held pride of place, rather as it did in (especially Western) Christianity. But the Sunni Islam to which Ahmad was devoted was primarily a religion of law. Whereas a Christian is likely to approach God as a forgiven sinner and a Hindu as a proud host, a Sunni Muslim goes to God as an obedient servant. The chief need is to find out one's duty and then to do it; that is, to elaborate and execute the law. I think this is the principal source of the personal dignity that is repeatedly identified as the distinguishing characteristic of devout Muslims: they know their duty and do it, unlike hand-wringing Christians who continually lament their inability to live as they ought.

By Ahmad's time, the die was probably cast: outside Shi'i circles, the effective majority recognized that the principal responsibility of Muslim religious leaders was to describe how to lead a God-pleasing life, which is to say the law. Accordingly, even the Mu'tazilah devoted considerable attention to the law. But how were people to know what the law was? First, how much was one to depend on the Qur'an? Liturgically, the Qur'an is important for all Muslims, unlike hadith. The word *qur'an* means "a recitation." Every Muslim recites some passages of it at every ritual prayer, pious Muslims memorized all of it (it is about two-thirds as long as the New Testament in Arabic), it is continuously recited aloud in the mosque and broadcast by radio, and even non-Arabophone Muslims enjoy reading through the Arabic. None of this applies to the hadith. When defining the law, the Qur'an is theoretically weightier than hadith, even in Sunni Islam and especially in modern expositions. It evidently seems more difficult today than it did a thousand years ago to base one's religion on such a nebulous body of information as the hadith, which only experts have command: much easier to stress one volume revealed from Heaven.

None the less, even the most cursory look at Islamic law shows that most of the rules are based on hadith. In the Middle Ages, the case for relying on hadith was often put in terms of an argument over how to occupy oneself in the mosque, with mistaken Puritan being shown that the Qur'an alone was not enough. This is an example from the Basran, 'Imran ibn al-Husayn (died 52/672?):

> A man came to him and asked him about something. He related to him some hadith. The man said, "Relate to us of the Book of God. Do not relate to us anything else". He said, "You are foolish. Do you find in the Book of God that the afternoon prayer comprises four [sets of bowings], during which one does not recite aloud? The number of prayers, the amount of the alms tax and so on? Do you find this explained in the Book of God? God has decreed all this and the *sunnah* explains it"
>
> (Ibn al-Mubarak, 143; sim., *Lisan* 1:3)

In other words, however helpful the Qur'an to his devotional life, the man had to realize that the hadith were necessary for him to know his essential duties, since only then could he understand the *sunnah*, the normative precedent laid down by the Prophet. A minor but typical example of going by hadith is observable during Ramadan in a country where most of the people are Muslim: the Qur'an states that the fast begins when a black thread can be distinguished from a white one but Muslims actually fast from the call to prayer at dawn to the call at sunset. This is because hadith expressly substitutes the call to prayer (*adhan*) for the thread test. The Khawarij and Mu'tazilah argued in the eighth and ninth centuries for a basis in Qur'an only, Ahmad and the Sunni party for hadith: the Sunni argument won.

The principal disagreement Ahmad referred to was to do with how much to depend on reason, how much on revelation and long-standing tradition. The principal term for "reason" is *ra'y*, literally meaning "opinion." It may seem unfair for one side to be labelled the adherents of mere opinion, but it is clear that *ra'y* originally meant "sound and considered opinion." It may have acquired the negative connotation of "mere opinion" because of Sunni polemics. (In rather the same way, "opinion" today retains a positive connotation in some contexts; for example, "Today, the Supreme Court issued its opinion ....") Adherents of *ra'y* contemporary with Ahmad liked to ask hypothetical questions to establish the logic of the law, to justify rules by appeal to equity or practicality, and to find rules for new cases by analogy with known cases, not by searching ever further for relevant hadith.

The Sunni party, to which Ahmad adhered, defined itself by its loyalty to the *sunnah*; that is, to normative precedent. For the law, this meant reliance on hadith; that is, on reports of what the Prophet and other early Muslims had said and done. The main advantage of adherence to *sunnah* was religious: it meant that people did not conceitedly rely on themselves but on older, wiser persons, closer to the Prophet and divine inspiration. The Basran, al-Sha'bi (d. 105/723–4?), answered a request for his opinion with the exclamation, "What will you do with my opinion? Piss on my opinion" (Ibn Sa'd 7/2:16 7:250). Adherence to *sunnah* was also thought to mean that people were not subject to capricious change of opinion. Ahmad quoted Malik (d. 179/795) as warning, "Every time we come across a man who argues better than another, shall we reject what Gabriel brought to the Prophet?" (*'Ilal* 2:72 1:228).

Reliance on precedent sometimes made Sunni law seem crudely irrational. However, that very irrationality might be proudly acknowledged as evidence that the Sunni jurisprudents were loyal to a transcendent God whose ways were not of the world. This is a famous dialogue between Malik's teacher Rabi'at al-Ra'y (died 136/753–4?) and Sa'id ibn al-Musayyab (died 94/712–13) over the compensation due for destroying a woman's fingers.

> "How much is it for a woman's finger?" "Ten camels", answered Sa'id. "How much for two fingers?" "Twenty camels". "How much for three?" "Thirty camels". "How much for four?" "Twenty camels". "When her injury is greater and her affliction more severe, her compensation diminishes?" "Are you an Iraqi? ... It's the *sunnah*, nephew."

(*Muw*. Yahya, *'uqul* 11)

At four fingers, the rule comes into effect that the compensation due to women is half that due to men – a rule that applies to all injuries for which the total compensation is a third or more of the one hundred camels that compensate for a man's life. ("Are you an Iraqi?" shows how the Medinans thought the Iraqis based their law on *ra'y*, whereas they were faithful to the *sunnah* – a conceit Ahmad seems to have endorsed only weakly, if at all.)

A division of opinion highly visible to twentieth-century scholarship is that between the hadith and local practice. Malik's *Muwatta'* continually adduces the practice of the people of Medina in particular to establish the *sunnah*. A famous example is the problem of option: according to most jurisprudents, either a buyer or a seller may annul a sale for any reason, so long as they are still together. Faulty merchandise may be returned for a refund but once buyer and seller have parted, there must be a noticeable fault. Jurisprudents cite a prophetic hadith report stating precisely this as the basis of the rule: "Buyer and seller are at option so long as they have not parted." Malik quotes the hadith report but dismisses it in favor of Medinan practice, which is to allow a sale to be annulled only for a fault, even when buyer and seller are still together (*Muw.*Yahya, *buyu'* 38).

Medinan practice was sometimes defended as a more reliable indication than the hadith of what the Prophet and his Companions used to do. Rabi'at al-Ra'y said: "A thousand from a thousand is better than one from one" (*Hilyah* 3:261). Ahmad was unimpressed by the citing of Medinan practice as an argument. On option, he quoted another Medinan, Ibn Abi Dhi'b (died 159/775–6?), who said Malik ought to be asked to repent of such an opinion and beheaded if he refused (*'Ilal* 1:539 *1:198*). In general, Ahmad inveighed against *ra'y* and specifically disparaged Malik for speaking by it; it was Shafi'i, not, so far as I know, Ahmad, who vigorously argued against Malik expressly for relying on Medinan practice.

Ahmad's comments on the big names of Islamic jurisprudence, as quoted by his immediate followers, tend to be negative. From Abu Dawud, for example, we hear, "There is no one but that his opinion is sometimes to be taken and sometimes left, except for the Prophet" (AD, 276). Abu Dawud asked Ahmad whether al-Awza'i (a famous Syrian jurisprudent) was any more worth following than Malik. He replied, "Don't give authority in your faith to any of those: what has come from the Prophet, take that" (AD, 277) and "I don't like Malik's opinion or anyone's opinion" (AD, 275). At most, Ahmad expressed a grudging preference for the professedly hadith-based jurisprudence of the Hijaz (Mecca and Medina) over the more sophisticated jurisprudence of Iraq. Ibn Hani' asked him whether he preferred the books of Shafi'i and Malik or of Abu Hanifah and AbuYusuf. He said:

I prefer al-Shafi'i, even though he composed a book. These give judicial opinions on the basis of hadith, whereas those give judicial opinions on the basis of *ra'y*. What a difference there is between them.

(Ibn Hani', 2:164)

Ahmad is frequently quoted against the writing of books of law. On being asked about a certain man who had written a book, Ahmad said, "Ask him whether any of the Companions of the Prophet did this, or any of the Followers." He then became angry. "Forbid the people (to pay attention to this book): incumbent on you is hadith" (Ibn Hani', 2:165). 'Abd Allah recalled his father as saying,

This Abu Hanifah wrote a book, then Abu Yusuf came and wrote a book, then Muhammad ibn al-Hasan (al-Shaybani) came and wrote a book – there is no end to this. Whenever a man comes along, he writes a book. This Malik wrote a book, al-Shafi'i came and wrote a book, too, and this one, meaning Abu Thawr has come and written a book. These books that he has written are an innovation. Whenever a man comes along, he writes a book and abandons the hadith of the Messenger of God.

('Al., 437)

Ahmad did allow that there was no harm in transcribing debates, especially to publish the hadith someone knew or to record judicial opinions.

It was presumably under this dispensation that Ahmad allowed disciples to transcribe his talk, though he was sometimes uneasy about it. A student said to him, "I want to write down these *masa'il* (legal problems), for fear I should forget." Ahmad told him, "Do not write a thing, for I dislike that my opinion (*ra'y*) be written down." Another time, he sensed that someone was writing and had slates in his sleeve. "Do not write down my opinion," he said, "for I may say something now concerning a juridical problem, then tomorrow go back on it" (IAY, 1:39). Following Ahmad's logic, contradictions among different *masa'il* collections do not show that his words have been mis-remembered; rather, contradictions are just what we should expect of accurate transcriptions. His leading disciple Abu Bakr al-Marrudhi recalled:

> I saw a Khurasani who had come to Abu 'Abd Allah and given him a fascicle. Abu 'Abd Allah looked into it and lo, it contained talk of his. He became angry and threw the book from his hand.

> (*Manaqib*, 194 265–6).

HANBALI LITERATURE

We know Ahmad's doctrines mainly through the writings of his disciples. Practically everything published in his name was actually put together by the next generation. During Ahmad's lifetime, learned Muslims were beginning the transition from oral transmission and personal notebooks to writing books they expected to be published intact and unchanged. According to Gregor Schoeler, among the first authors deliberately to write books for publication were the mid-ninth century littérateurs al-Jahiz (died 255/868–9) and al-Mada'ini (died 228/842–3?). People tend to be especially conservative in religious matters, and there is good evidence that specifically Islamic literature continued to be disseminated in the older style, as lecture notes, subject to variation from one note-taker to another and (though the extent to which it happened is controversial) to editorial re-arrangement, abridgement, expansion, and rewording.

Compare the literary bases of the other Sunni schools. Malik's *Muwatta'* is usually taken as the earliest surviving

account of Maliki law but it took some time for the text to
crystallize. And it was never the chief literary basis of the
Maliki school: medieval Maliki writers usually identify that as
another collection of Malik's opinions, with additions, made
by Ibn al-Qasim (died 191/806). Where there were contradictions, Ibn al-Qasim's account was preferred to the *Muwatta'*.
However, this does not mean exactly that the Malikiyah allowed
Ibn al-Qasim to overrule Malik: there were always compet-
ing versions of Malik's opinion. Over a hundred scholars are
named as transmitting the *Muwatta'*. Twelfth-century scholars
had access to several dozen versions. Modern scholars have
access to six or seven, of which just two or three are complete
– the rest are fragments. A comparison of the different versions
shows strong similarities, but they address topics in different
orders, one version may cite a hadith report backing up Malik's
opinion, where another presents just the opinion, and so on.
There are also signs of what textual critics call "interference,"
when medieval copyists put different versions next to each
other and adjusted their texts accordingly. The version by
Muhammad al-Shaybani (died 189/804–5), who was active
mainly in Baghdad, expressly refers to that of Yahya ibn Yahya
(died 234/849?) of Cordova. Other versions may have been
recast on comparison with others, without express acknowl-
edgement. A good century after Malik's death, there was still
considerable instability in the formulation of his opinions.

The Hanafi school is named for Abu Hanifah, but no one
published books in his name; rather his opinions are known
almost entirely from books published in the names of his
disciples Abu Yusuf, under whom Ahmad briefly studied, and
Shaybani. It is even controversial to what extent the books
appearing under their names are actually the work of Abu Yusuf
and Shaybani; that is, to what degree they have been reworked
by later adherents. One obvious indication of reworking is

the way parts of the texts refer to Abu Yusuf and Shaybani in the third person. A subtler indication is how different works address the same problems in dissimilar ways. There is also the phenomenon of the commentaries on Shaybani's works, which appear from the late ninth century onwards. Why should the stream of commentaries have begun only a century after his death? It makes better sense if we regard the commentaries as succeeding pseudonymous reworkings; that is, for most of the ninth century, the way to elaborate on Shaybani's teaching was to write as if he were speaking.

Pseudonymous reworking is more easily demonstrable in Shafi'i's works, since we are able to compare a somewhat wider range of extant, contemporary witnesses to his opinions than we are to Abu Yusuf's and Shaybani's. The earliest commentary on Shafi'i's writings is the *Mukhtasar* of al-Muzani (died 264/877?), who is said to have studied under Shafi'i in his twenties. The *Mukhtasar* combines quotation, paraphrase and commentary (Muzani sometimes presumes to disagree with his master). Close examination of the *Mukhtasar* shows that a great deal of what purports to be quotation must actually be paraphrasing or extrapolation; that is, they reflect Muzani's guess as to what Shafi'i would have said had he still been alive to answer questions. Comparison with other quotations of Shafi'i shows that all the leading sources are similar mixtures.

What about books purporting to quote Ahmad ibn Hanbal? These are principally the *masa'il* collections, the earliest and best source for his opinions on legal questions. They do not purport to be his very writings, as the works of Abu Yusuf and Shaybani purport to be theirs. They are much more consistent than the putative works of Shafi'i, which include expository prose and dialogue, long quotations from Shafi'i, and short comments from compilers. The *masa'il* purport to record series of short statements, either responses to questions from

the compilers or responses to questions from others that the
compilers overheard. Most are thematically arranged (Salih's
appears to be random), but otherwise, there is little evidence
of editorial intervention.

The next stage of Hanbali literary development was the
synthesis, in the last third of the ninth century, of all the available *masa'il* collections (fifty-six transmitters are named) by
Abu Bakr al-Khallal. This was followed by the composition
of the first epitome (*mukhtasar*) of Hanbali law by al-Khiraqi
(died 334/945–6), although we do not know whether his work
depended on Khallal's. The Hanbali school seems to have largely
skipped the stage of commenting on the eponym's doctrine by
the paraphrase and extrapolation evident (in descending order
of certainty) in Shafi'i, Hanafi and Maliki literature.

The *masa'il* collections seem much truer to life than books
from other schools. None of the others – Malik, Abu Yusuf,
Shaybani, or Shafi'i – expresses uncertainty so often. For
example: "I heard Ahmad asked about a man who performs
some elements of his ritual ablution three times, other elements twice. He said, 'I hope it discharges his duty'" (AD, 6–7).
Equally typically: "I heard Ahmad asked about the buying and
selling of fox skins. He said, 'I don't know'" (AD, 193). Contradictions among the *masa'il* are almost always a matter of
degree. For example, a dictum from Ibn Hani' states: "I heard
him say, 'It does not please me that a man should wear a turban
in prayer that does not go at all below his throat. It is related
of Tawus that he disliked it'" (Ibn Hani', 1:58). This opinion is
supported by the opinion of a Yemeni Follower. In contrast,
'Abd Allah said: "My father said, 'It is disliked that a man should
wear a turban without letting any of it go below his throat.'
He said, 'This is Satan's turban'"('Al., 449). It seems stronger
to identify a clothing style with Satan than simply to say that a
Follower disliked it. However, the legal category of the turban

that does not hang down is unchanged from one collection to the other: it is disliked without being outright forbidden.

To sum up, I am inclined to place much more confidence in the *masa'il* collections as accurate transcriptions of what Ahmad said than in the early works of other schools as accurate transcriptions of what Abu Hanifah and his followers, Malik and Shafi'i said. They are late enough to belong to the period of exact recopying, as opposed to creative reworking; contradictions from book to book are much harder to find and the continual record of uncertainty and tentativeness is unparalleled: the other works purport to transcribe speech but almost never with the verisimilitude of the *masa'il* collections.

AHMAD'S JURISPRUDENCE

Perhaps the earliest surviving notice of a division between *ra'y* and hadith is an essay by a courtier, Ibn al-Muqaffa', written in the third quarter of the eighth century (thus before Ahmad was born). This essay criticizes those who refer to the hadith for an apparent contradiction: that what they call *sunnah* was the *ra'y* of an earlier generation. In a huge collection of hadith by Ahmad's shaykh 'Abd al-Razzaq (died 211/827), scarcely one item in five goes back to the Prophet. The opinions of Companions and Followers (Followers met Companions but not the Prophet) form most of the collection. In Malik's *Muwatta'*, the Companion and Follower hadith outnumber the Prophetic and the opinion of a Follower is occasionally allowed to overrule that of a Companion (although never of the Prophet, so far as I have noticed).

In theory, Ahmad avoided the criticism by pushing back the authoritative *sunnah* to the first generation, the Prophet's Companions, or even to a few of the Companions alone. Abu Dawud (an important traditionist) recalled,

> I heard Ahmad say when a man had asked, "If there is
> hadith [literally, if something has come] from the Followers
> concerning something about which there is nothing from the
> Prophet, does one have to go by it?" He said, "No but there is
> scarcely anything not covered by hadith from the Companions
> of the Prophet, meaning something that to me resembles that
> thing".

(AD, 276–7)

Ahmad thus concedes that the opinions of Followers are liable
to be as mistaken as anyone else's but he thinks the tradition
must hold an answer to every question, without the need to
appeal to present-day reasoning. In his talk of resemblance, he
advocates reasoning by analogy without expressly calling it so,
since it was his adversaries, the adherents of *ra'y,* who expressly
called their method "analogy" (*qiyas*).

Ahmad sometimes accepted a definition of *sunnah* as narrow
as the practice of the Prophet and the first four caliphs. Abu
Dawud again:

> I more than once heard Ahmad, when he had been asked
> whether the practice of Abu Bakr, 'Umar, 'Uthman and 'Ali
> was *sunnah*. He said, "Yes". Once he said, "On account of the
> hadith report of the Messenger of God: 'Incumbent on you is
> my *sunnah* and the *sunnah* of the Rightly Guided Caliphs.' He
> thus named it *sunnah*."

Asked whether the dicta of other persons such as Abu Mu'adh
and Ibn Mas'ud, other Companions, equally constituted *sunnah*,
Ahmad said "I will not deny it, and I dislike to disagree with
any of them" (AD, 277). This is a much wider definition than
Shafi'i's, which tends to restrict the authoritative *sunnah* to the
dictum and example of the Prophet alone. (It is also notably
reticent about jurisprudence: Ahmad was always uncomfortable with theorizing.)

In practice, Ahmad did sometimes cite as *sunnah* what looks like the *ra'y* of an earlier generation. Concerning the question of whether a pilgrim may go to Mecca carrying weapons, he related (with full *isnad*) that the two Basrans, al-Hasan (died 110/728) and Muhammad ibn Sirin (died 110/729) had seen no harm in it (AD, 11–12). In these and other instances, he used a verb (*yarayani*) related to *ra'y*. Citing al-Hasan and Muhammad ibn Sirin in this way agrees with the normal style of jurisprudence in the eighth century, so far as we can make it out from ninth-century sources. However, it does not agree so well with Ahmad's professed theory.

A little more often, Ahmad cites the opinion of a Companion. Concerning another question of the pilgrimage to Mecca, he quotes (with full *isnad*) the report of the Basran, Hafsah bint Sirin (died after 100/718–9), "They used to like to descend at Khayf al-Ayman by Mina," which presumably means the Companions in general (AD, 121–2). A second example: if there is no water suitable for making ritual ablutions, dust may be used instead, a procedure called *tayammum*. Of this, Ahmad said, "There is no harm in someone's leading the prayer on performing the *tayammum* even though those led have performed the normal minor ritual ablution. Ibn 'Abbas led the prayer after he had performed the *tayammum*" ('Al., 143). This is to cite a Companion's example as authoritative. Another example of Ahmad's relying on a hadith report going back only to a Companion: "I asked, 'If the Khawarij [violent early Muslim sectarians] overcome a people and collect from them the alms tax on their wealth, does that discharge their duty [to pay the alms tax]?' He said, 'It is related concerning this [question] of Ibn 'Umar that he said it discharged their duty.' I said, 'Is this what you go for?' He said, 'I tell you what Ibn 'Umar said about it and you ask me if this is what I go for?'" (Ibn Hani', 1:115). He would not presume to disagree with a Companion.

The hardest part about inferring the law from the hadith is that the reports are often contradictory. For Ahmad, contradiction was normally an indication that somewhere, someone had misquoted, whether knowingly or not. This is why he insisted that knowledge of hadith was a necessary qualification for giving juridical opinions: not only were the rules to be inferred from hadith (as opposed to, say, current convenience) but unsound hadith reports could be eliminated from consideration only by the comparison of numerous variants. He was asked: "How many hadith reports will suffice a man to give juridical opinions? Will 100,000 suffice?" "No." "200,000?" "No." "300,000?" "No." "400,000?" "No." "500,000?" "I hope so." (IAY, 1:131, 141). It was not that, amongst half a million different hadith reports, there must be something to cover every situation but rather, with most of the half-million being the same as other reports but with variant *isnad*s, knowing half a million would make possible proper hadith criticism and thus the identification of the reliable ones.

Sometimes Ahmad resorted to a rough test of preponderance. For example, "I heard Abu 'Abd Allah say concerning the *nabbash* (grave robber), 'Most hadith reports [say] to cut off [his hand]. I think one should cut'"(Ibn Hani', 2:89; some jurisprudents doubted whether the coffin and grave clothes were actually anyone's property and hence could be stolen). More often, he gave his own opinion, without supporting evidence. For example, from 'Abd Allah: "I asked my father about dirhams. He said, 'There is no harm in touching them when one is not in a state of ritual purity'" ('Al., 111). A particularly scrupulous Muslim might fear to touch them, on the grounds that they bore Qur'anic quotations and people in a state of ritual impurity should not touch the Qur'an. From Salih: "I asked, 'May someone fasting sniff perfume?' He said, 'Yes'" (Salih, 6). Again from Salih: "I said, 'What do you say of a poor woman I have in my house? I am often given something for [distribution to] the poor, so I give some to her when I divide it among the poor.' He said, 'One should not be partial to her in that. One should give to her as one gives to others'" (Salih, 560).

Ahmad sometimes used the language of *ra'y*; for example, from Salih, "I think (*ara*) that a man may will [money for the vicarious performance of] the pilgrimage but I dislike that a man should take a wage for performing a good work" (Salih, 1084). Often, a modest tentativeness suggests his opinion had no clear basis in hadith. For example, 'Abd Allah records that, asked whether someone in a state of major ritual impurity may give the call to prayer, Ahmad said, "It does not please me." 'Abd Allah then asked his father, "What if a man is in a state of minor ritual impurity?" To this, Ahmad said, "I hope there is no harm in it" ('Al., 57–8). Similarly, 'Abd Allah says:

> I read aloud before my father, saying, "What if a woman prays with some of her hair exposed, or part of her lower leg or part of her forearm?". He said, "It does not please me". "So what if she has finished praying?". He said, "If it just a little, I hope [it is acceptable]."

('Al., 63)

Occasionally, his reported reasoning is intricate. Ahmad is quoted at length on the case of a man who contracts a marriage with an infant, who is then nursed by his wife or concubine (Salih, 500). Does it matter whether he has had sexual relations with the nursing woman? What if the mother of his wife or concubine nurses the infant? What are the implications for the bride price he has paid to become engaged to the infant? How long must pass before the nursing woman and infant may be married to someone else? This laying out of the law by proposing a hypothetical case and then systematically going

over it is practically indistinguishable from what we find in
the books of Shafiʻi, Shaybani and others Ahmad disparaged as
depending on *ra'y*.

Sometimes, it can be demonstrated that Ahmad's opinion
was directly based on traditional evidence. Under Islamic law,
travellers are not required to observe the Ramadan fast but
are allowed to eat and drink by daylight and make up the days
missed when they have stopped travelling. Ibn Hani' reports,
"I heard him say, 'Breaking the fast is the latter of two com-
mands from the Prophet .... Whoever fasts in travelling need
not make it up.' Another time he said, 'Breaking the fast is
preferable to us. If he fasts, it discharges his duty'" (Ibn Hani',
1:129). Ahmad was aware of two contradictory but sound
hadith reports from the Prophet concerning this question. He
accepted that one identifiably recorded a later saying of the
Prophet's and therefore abrogated the first. Ahmad's second
saying looks like mere *ra'y* but we are fortunate that Ibn Hani'
heard Ahmad explain his reasoning at another time and so
we see, at least partly, the basis for what Ahmad said: chiefly
prophetic hadith.

Finally, there are occasions when Ahmad's personal example
demonstrates the law. This is the old style of taking the shaykh's
practice as an indication of the law, which pervades the *Musannaf* of Ahmad's teacher ʻAbd al-Razzaq. For example, a section
on raising the hands in the ritual prayer presents successive
reports of how a Companion raised his hands, how a Follower
raised his hands, how three Companions raised their hands, a
Follower's dictum, and finally the observation that this Follower had been seen raising his hands in conformity with his
dictum. ʻAbd Allah ibn Ahmad says,

> I asked my father about a man who prays the ritual prayers
> at home, whether he must call to prayer and announce that

the prayer is about to begin. He said, "There is no harm in his calling to prayer. If he lets the call to prayer of the people of the city suffice, then that suffices for him". I used to pray with my father, he and I together, while he was hiding. He would call to prayer and announce that the prayer was about to begin, then we would pray together.

('Al., 61)

Thus we see which option Ahmad chose (despite the risk of discovery), having pronounced both equally valid in theory. Ibn Hani' reports, "I saw Abu 'Abd Allah spit between his feet in prayer. I saw him spit in the course of the ritual prayer, the supererogatory" (Ibn Hani', 1:43). This shows that spitting does not invalidate a ritual prayer. I have come across no example of the shaykh's example as authoritative evidence later than these earliest Hanbali books.

Ahmad's responses to questions were often imprecise, or careless of the distinction between "required" and "recommended." Consider this exchange between Ahmad and his son 'Abd Allah:

He said, 'I read before my father, "What is the least one must recite of the Qur'an to discharge one's duty in the ritual prayer?". He said, "The opening of the Book and a chapter.". I said, "What if one recites the opening of the Book by itself?". He said, "That discharges one's duty"'.

('Al., 77)

Had 'Abd Allah not added his own question to the one he found in writing (that is, that someone else had asked), we might have been left with the impression that the opening chapter alone was not enough. Actually, it seems to be the minimum permissible: that and another chapter rather make up the *recommended* minimum.

Ahmad thus adduced a great many different sorts of evidence in support of his opinions, including examples and dicta from Followers, Companions, the Right-Guided Caliphs and the Prophet. Two-thirds of the time (in most of the *masa'il* collections and considerably more in that of Ibn Hani'), he gives his own opinion, without evidence. A later Hanbali writer, Ibn Qayyim al-Jawziyah (died Damascus, 751/1350), summarizes Ahmad's sources, in descending order of importance, as:

1) well-attested prophetic hadith, ignoring contrary opinions from Companions and claims of *ijma'* (consensus) to the contrary;

2) the well-attested opinions of the Prophet's Companions;

3) if the Companions disagreed, whichever opinion was closest to the Qur'an and prophetic *sunnah*;

4) weakly-attested prophetic hadith, mainly *mursal* (in which a Follower reports what the Prophet said, without naming his source);

5) *qiyas* (analogy).

(*I'lam* 1:24–6)

This seems roughly correct. It is suitably different from the Shafi'i scheme (so often presented as the essential basis of Islamic law): Qur'an, prophetic *sunnah*, *ijma'* and *qiyas*. However, Ibn Qayyim al-Jawziyah's concern was to present Ahmad as a great jurisprudent not so different from the eponyms of the other great schools of law. His list is no guide at all to what evidence Ahmad most often cites, as recorded in the *masa'il* collections, nor does it acknowledge the peculiarly religious quality of Ahmad's doctrine.

Susan Spectorsky summarizes Ahmad's method (especially as exemplified in the *masa'il* collection of Abu Dawud) thus:

Ibn Hanbal readily answers questions on non-controversial matters but whenever he knows of conflicting traditions or conflicting opinion, he refuses to risk allowing his own answer to become authoritative. In fact, he answers all questions in terms of traditional criticism. If he cannot answer a question satisfactorily within the framework of traditions, he prefers not to answer at all.

(*Fiqh*, 461).

This is more satisfactory, although it exaggerates Ahmad's consistency: he does risk allowing his answer to become authoritative and does not always refrain from overruling conflicting opinion. However, for the most part, the pious concern to do right and not impose his own reasoning shines through Ahmad's doctrine more than almost any comparable body of quotations from any other early Muslim jurisprudent. Spectorsky brings out his morality, in contrast to the more technical legal reasoning of his contemporary Ishaq ibn Rahawayh, particularly regarding marriage and divorce:

It also becomes clear, despite inconsistencies, that there is a moral dimension to Ibn Hanbal's responses: he gives preference to doctrines that protect women from exploitation, condemns the use of *hiyal* (legal stratagems) and requires actions and words to have consequences for which the doers and speakers are responsible.

(*Chapters*, 7)

Ahmad's juridical opinions always had a certain improvised character. He worked when the culture of exact recording and transmission was just beginning. In some ways, he actively promoted exact transmission, as when he encouraged the use of notebooks, not memory, but he was also part of the earlier culture of oral transmission and permanent flexibility, when it was hard to challenge what anyone said on the grounds that it disagreed with what had been written. The *masa'il* collections show both sides.

THE HANBALI SCHOOL OF LAW

Disliking to see his own opinions recorded and urging no one to follow any jurisprudent of the recent past, Ahmad disapproved of the whole idea of a school of law, wherein the opinions of some famous historical jurisprudent are elaborated but almost never contradicted. According to Shafi'i accounts, Ahmad was his disciple in Baghdad, before Shafi'i moved on to Old Cairo, and some modern scholars have hastily assumed that there was little significant difference between their methods. However, Hanbali accounts of their relationship are significantly cooler, and the *masa'il* collections seem quite different from the works attributed to Shafi'i. Shafi'i's continual return to questions of method and refutation of other schools have no parallels in the *masa'il* collections, while Ahmad's morality and hadith criticism have no parallels in the works of Shafi'i.

The first stages of the formation of a Hanbali school (as opposed to one man with his own opinions) have been mentioned already: the recording of Ahmad's opinions by various disciples, the synthesis of most collections by Khallal, and the distillation of those opinions by Khiraqi into a succinct code. In the work of the qadi Abu Ya'la ibn al-Farra' (died Baghdad, 458/1065), the Hanbali school acquired a tradition of proper jurisprudence (*usul al-fiqh*). Given that Ahmad was uneasy with the recording of his opinions, he would presumably have liked each successive stage even less.

As some Hanabilah (adherents of the Hanbali school) were bringing their practice into line with that of the other Sunni schools of law, other Hanabilah were rioting. Some are said to have prevented a public funeral for the renunciant al-Muhasibi (who died, probably in Baghdad, in 243/857–8), whose theological speculation Ahmad had vigorously condemned; others did the same for the jurisprudent, Qur'an commentator, and historian, al-Tabari (died Baghdad, 310/923), who also espoused views repugnant to the Hanabilah (although there are four or five versions of exactly which view provoked the siege of his house). Several times in the 320s/930s, Hanabilah broke musical instruments, beat singing girls, organised the stoning of Shafi'iyah at the mosques and molested Shi'ah visiting the tombs of their martyrs. After the Buyids occupied Baghdad in 334/945, the Hanabilah were particularly associated with anti-Shi'i rioting. In the eleventh century, they were major allies of the caliphs in Baghdad, as they struggled to wrest back power from various warlords (until the 1050s mainly the Buyids, followed by the Seljuqs).

During the eleventh and twelfth centuries, the caliphs became temporal rulers again but their authority was largely restricted to Iraq. The Hanbali school prospered in Baghdad but seems to have disappeared from the cities of Iran. One major Hanbali jurisprudent, Ibn Hubayrah (died 560/1165), was vizier to two caliphs, while Hanbali rioters dealt the final blow to Seljuq authority in 1175. However, Baghdad's cultural importance was by now no greater than that of other cities, such as Damascus and Cairo, and it diminished even more when, in 1258, the Mongols killed the caliph and massacred most of the people. Baghdad practically disappeared from the cultural map after Tamerlane's massacre in 1401. Hanbalism survived in Damascus, thanks to a series of Syrian Hanabilah, who traveled to Baghdad in the later twelfth century and brought back its learning. Ibn Qudamah (died Damascus, 620/1223) was the most important of them. However, his

writings have a significant admixture of Shafi'i doctrine,
extending even to plagiarism of Shafi'i works. This was how
Hanbalism survived until modern times, as a school of law
parallel to other schools. It might have died out, like some
other schools (for example, those named after Abu Thawr,
Dawud al-Zahiri, and al-Tabari, which flourished for a time
in the tenth and eleventh centuries), had it not become more
like the others. However, Ahmad ibn Hanbal certainly wanted
nothing like the others.

Many educated Muslims today want to strip away the medieval scholastic tradition and go back to the raw material of
revelation, to the rules God wants. "Salafi" is the current term
for this tendency. They are impatient with the clever discus-
sions and indeterminacy of medieval handbooks. Their program
sounds similar to Ahmad's: it would not have bothered him that
modern Salafiyah are more likely to identify their program
with Ibn Qudamah's grandson, Ibn Taymiyah (died Damascus,
728/1328), than with Ahmad himself.

To me, the great difference between Ahmad and today's
Salafiyah appears to be his substantial acquaintance with hadith
and his full appreciation of how vast it is and ultimately how
intractable. One would not be surprised to hear a Salafi say,
"Forbid the people to pay attention to this book", but it is less
easy to imagine one saying, again and again, "I don't know."

4

CORRECT BELIEF

"Correct belief" was crucially important to Ahmad and the Sunni Islam he espoused. This chapter was once going to be called *Theology,* but Ahmad does not so much elaborate, explain and defend correct belief as succinctly declare what it is. In theology – the knowledge of divinity – Ahmad thought Muslims should unite around a fairly minimal set of propositions. Modern Arab Christians translate "theology" as *'ilm al-lahut.* The nearest ninth-century equivalent, *kalam,* designates something Ahmad did not want.

The main sources for this chapter are Ahmad's six creeds. Seven creeds, of varying length, said to have been dictated by Ahmad, are quoted in the biographical dictionary of Ibn Abi Ya'la (died 526/1133). Henri Laoust, followed by other modern scholars, viewed them as syntheses of Ahmad's pronouncements by the school rather than deliberate compositions by Ahmad himself. This is certainly possible. One of the shorter creeds is presented in two versions, with minor variations, and so must go back to a common source; however, that source is not necessarily Ahmad. The creeds are mutually contradictory as to whether 'Ali is to be preferred to other Companions. These contradictions probably reflect inconsistencies in what Ahmad said at different times, but we cannot rule out reworking by various followers, each with his own slightly different view of Ahmad's position. The crude style of the creeds – repetition, nothing more than simple arguments, and shifts into the second person and between singular and plural – seems credibly oral and improvised. Their archaic vocabulary (for example, *hadith* and *athar* are used interchangeably) favors their being at least very near to Ahmad's time.

WHO IS IN, WHO IS OUT?

Judaism has famously been distinguished as a religion of ortho-*praxy* and Christianity as a religion of ortho*doxy*. That is, the reasoning goes, Jews on the inside and non-Jews on the outside are mainly distinguished by what they *do*, while Christians on the inside and non-Christians on the outside are mainly distinguished by what they *believe*. Sa'adiah Gaon (died 942) listed what would cause a person to stop being a Jew: the list comprises only works, such as violating the Sabbath and not fasting on the Day of Atonement. Material for a doctrine of inclusion or exclusion according to actions can be found in the New Testament; for example, "Not every one that saith unto me, Lord, Lord, shall enter into the kingdom of heaven; but he that doeth the will of my Father which is in heaven" (Matt. 7:21). Nevertheless, the bell, book, and candle of excommunication from Christianity have only ever been brought out for doctrinal offenses such as denying the Trinity, not for crimes such as adultery and murder, nor (in contrast to Sa'adiah's list) for ritual offences such as not going to church and not fasting in Lent.

Islam is often classified, like Judaism, as a religion of ortho-praxy – and not without reason: as with Judaism, Islam's chief expression of faithfulness is obedience to the revealed law; like Jewish rabbis, Muslim men of religion, the ulema, are experts in the law, and like Jews, Muslims are not divided by recondite theological questions (such as whether Christ has both a divine and a human nature or one human and divine nature) into a multifarious array of churches.

Questions of law undoubtedly seem more important to Muslims than Christians. I have more than once witnessed a conversation between an Evangelical Christian and a Muslim in which the Evangelical urged the Muslim to consider his status as a sinner. What was supposed to happen was that the Muslim realized that he was a sinner, unable to please God on his own, beg to be told how he could restore himself to divine favor, hear the good news that Christ will bear his sin for him, and so on. What actually happens is that the Muslim says yes, he sins but he also obeys, and at the final reckoning, God will generously let each act of obedience outweigh many sins. He goes away wondering why Christians are so morbidly obsessed with sin. Conversely, I have often been asked by Muslims how Christians divide inherited property. What is supposed to happen is that I realize I have a religion that does not provide for elementary demands of life, beg to be told how I may know what to do, and then hear that I need only convert to Islam and follow the Qur'an and God's Prophet. What actually happens is that we both go away wondering at the other's complacency. This mutual incomprehension comes about, at least in part, because Christians are used to thinking first of theology and Muslims of law.

Strictly, it is untrue that Sunni Islam (followed by the majority of Muslims) is orthopractic: it stands somewhere between Judaism and Christianity. The believing profession of loyalty – "There is no god but God and Muhammad is His messenger" – is what makes a Muslim, not practical obedience. Sectarian Khariji Muslims may have treated cardinal sinners as apostates but Ahmad desired a community of Muslims, not a Puritan sect considering only themselves believers (much less a sect perpetually at war with most professing Muslims):

One refrains [from casting aspersions on] the people of the
qiblah (those who pray toward Mecca). Do not call any of them
an unbeliever on account of a sin, nor exclude him from Islam
on account of a deed, unless there is a hadith report about that.

(Creed I, IAY, 1:27).

We do not call any monotheist an unbeliever, even if they
commit cardinal sins.

(Creed II, IAY, 1:130–1).

Whoever dies of the people of the *qiblah* professing to believe
in one god, he is to be prayed over and his forgiveness asked.
We do not refuse to pray over him on account of any sin he has
committed, whether small or great – that is up to God.

(Creed III, IAY, 1:246).

The believer of *ahl al-sunnah wa-al-jama'ah* ... does not call any
of the people of monotheism an unbeliever on account of a sin.

(Creed IV, IAY, 1:294).

We do not refuse to pray over anyone of the people of the
qiblah on account of any sin he has committed, whether small
or great, unless he is an innovator whom the Prophet has
excluded from Islam: the Qadariyah, the Murji'ah, the Rafidah,
and the Jahmiyah.

(Creed V, IAY, 1:311–12).

[We require] prayer over whoever dies of the people of this
qiblah, their reckoning being up to God.

(Creed VI, IAY, 1:344).

There is an orthopractic tinge to Sunni Islam: the law marks it as the saved community, so Muslims normally demonstrate that they belong to that community by observing the law, if not in every detail, at least to some extent, as defined by local custom. This tinge is a little deeper in Ahmad's theory than in majority Sunni doctrine. Only Ahmad and the Hanbali school after him identified a minimum level of observance; namely, the performance of the ritual prayer. Most Sunni schools of law regard not praying as a capital offense, but only the Hanbali calls for the execution of non-prayers as apostates. (By the thirteenth century, Hanbali jurisprudents admitted the offense was so common that it would be impractical to enforce any such rule.)

Whether all Muslims will be saved is another question. Since the tenth century, the classic Sunni teaching (as against the Mu'tazili) has been that they will be, if not directly by God's forgiveness, then indirectly by the Prophet's intercession. Ahmad's position was more cautious. It was dangerous to assume that one was saved. Ahmad quoted Sufyan al-Thawri, "We assume that people are believers when it comes to ordinances and inheritances and we hope they truly are. Yet we do not know our standing with God" (*Sunnah*, 73 *83*). That is, every nominal Muslim would receive the benefit of the doubt when it came to such matters as paying taxes (where non-Muslims faced an extra charge) and inheritance (which was forbidden between Muslims and non-Muslims), but only God knew whether any individiual Muslim was to be saved at the Last Judgement. In consequence, Ahmad strongly favored saying not "I am a believer" but "I am a believer, God willing" (Creed I, IAY 1:24). He was sure believers would be saved but it would have been presumptuous to suggest that anyone knew who, to God's mind, was a believer. We might regret the hectoring way he piles up authorities for "I am a believer, God willing" (for example *Sunnah*, 84 *94*) but we must respect his fear of complacency.

WHAT AHMAD BELIEVED

Ahmad's will, drawn up not long before he was summoned to
Samarra and reaffirmed on his deathbed, is quoted at length
in his son Salih's memoir, and so we can be certain about what
he positively believed (*Sirah*, 109):

> In the name of God, the Merciful, the Compassionate. This is
> the will of Ahmad ibn Muhammad ibn Hanbal.
> He wills that he testifies that there is no god but God alone,
> having no partner, and that Muhammad is his slave and
> messenger, whom he sent *with guidance and the religion of
> truth, to make it prevail over all [other] religion, no matter whether
> the polytheists dislike it* (Q. 61:9).
> He wills that whoever of his family and relations will obey him
> should worship God among the worshippers and praise him
> among the praisers and that they should show good faith
> toward the great majority of the Muslims.
> He wills, "I accept God as a lord, Islam as a religion and
> Muhammad as a prophet".
> He wills that I [*sic*] owe 'Abd Allah ibn Muhammad, known as
> Furan, about fifty dinars. He is to be believed in what he
> says. Let his claim be settled out of the yield of the house, if
> God wills. When he has taken what is his, my two sons Salih
> and 'Abd Allah ibn Ahmad ibn Muhammad ibn Hanbal are to
> give each male and female ten dirhams after Ibn Muhammad
> has taken what I owe him.

The creedal portion takes up more space than the disposi-
tion of his property. (The Qur'an famously prescribes une-
qual inheritance shares to sons and daughters, but the pre-
sumption in Islamic law is that gifts and bequests are divided
equally between the sexes, so there is nothing unconventional
about Ahmad's treating his grandsons and granddaughters the
same.)

It is a notably simple creed: to believe in God, Muhammad and Islam, without a word about the created nature of the Qur'an, the nature of God's attributes, and the other hotly debated theological topics of his day. For Ahmad, a complex theology was not a necessary part of religion.

REJECTED THEOLOGICAL PARTIES

Ahmad's creeds are mainly lists of propositions on which, against contrary opinion, he insists. Creed I concludes with a list of the parties Ahmad rejects, a little longer but not very different from lists in other creeds. First are the Murji'ah, those who say that faith is the profession of belief, without works (IAY, 1:31–2). They believed that either one had faith or one did not. To Ahmad, it seemed that someone who obeyed God on many points must be more faithful than someone who obeyed on only a few. He ridicules the Murji'ah for asserting that their faith is the same as that of the angels and prophets and that faith cannot increase or decrease. Abu Hanifah was pretty certainly an adherent of the Murji'ah, as were some of his followers but they seem to have disappeared at about Ahmad's time (although some of their ideas lived on under other names, even, arguably, becoming mainstream Sunni opinion).

Next are the Qadariyah, who believe in free will, not divine predestination (IAY, 1:32). We know more of this party, for texts advocating their position survive from the eighth century. They seem to have had two chief concerns. First, they wanted to persuade people to be better Muslims: many early Qadariyah were popular preachers. It made sense to think of people as having a choice to do better, else why preach at all? Second, they could not see how predestination was compatible with God's being completely good: how could God will that someone do an evil thing, or punish someone for doing a deed that He himself had ordained? For Ahmad, divine omnipotence required that every deed occur by God's will: could anyone say the fetus in the adulteress's womb had been created by the will of an adulterer, not God (IAY, 1:25–6)?

Third came the Mu'tazilah. Because he suffered under the Inquisition for insisting that the Qur'an was not part of creation, Ahmad is often alleged to have opposed the Mu'tazilah above all, since they held that it was. Actually, the Inquisition was not associated with the Mu'tazilah but rather with a particular Hanafi jurisprudent. When Ahmad inveighed against the people who believed in a created Qur'an, he called their sect (if he called it anything) the Jahmiyah and condemned it along with the adherents of ra'y, dialectic, and disputations (IAY, 1:342). Ahmad's express complaint about the Mu'tazilah was to do either with their lack of belief in various items found only in the hadith, not in the Qur'an (for example, in torment between death and the Last Judgment, in the Prophet's intercession for grave Muslim sinners, and in the Basin "a month's journey across, able to contain the number of the stars of heaven" that Believers will cross at the Last Judgment [IAY, 1:32, 242]) or what makes an unbeliever. According to the Mu'tazilah, Ahmad says, Adam was an unbeliever for disobeying God, Jacob's brothers were unbelievers for lying to their father, and anyone who steals a grain becomes an unbeliever (IAY, 1:343). He preferred to reserve "unbeliever" to describe people with wrong beliefs.

Fourth came the Nusayriyah, who are otherwise unknown. They were said to be Qadariyah, to assert that whoever steals a grain is an unbeliever, and to have similar opinions to the Khawarij. That nobody else mentions this group (the Nusayriyah of the later medieval and modern periods is an aberrant Syrian Shi'i group) and that one of their leading offences (that anyone who steals a grain becomes an unbeliever) is elsewhere attributed to another group indicates the polemical nature of Ahmad's creeds. These are not objective surveys, and it is more important to brand rejected views with strange names ("they have names not resembling those of the righteous and the learned" – IAY, 1:31) than to represent them as they would recognize themselves, somewhat as polemists of our time have spoken of "Communists," "Fascists," and "pseudo-intellectuals."

Next come the Jahmiyah (IAY, 1:32). No one is known to have identified himself as a member of this sect (except for one staunch Sunni who said he had defected from them: see Watt, 144). Ahmad lumps together, as adherents of the Jahmiyah, people who considered themselves sharply at odds with one another, most notably those who said that the Qur'an had been created, like everything else other than God, and those who said the Qur'an itself was not part of creation (his position) but conceded that it had appeared in time (that is, there had been a time when the Qur'an was not) or that the ink on the paper and the sounds of its recitation were created. This latter group considered themselves good adherents of the Sunnah, indeed its greatest defenders. Ahmad would have preferred to do without their rationalistic defense.

After the Jahmiyah come the Rafidah and various sub-sects (IAY, 1:33). Their offense was to exalt 'Ali above Abu Bakr and 'Umar, or simply above 'Uthman, Talhah, al-Zubayr, and 'A'ishah (the Zaydi position). In his anti-Shi'i polemics, Ahmad continually points out that they necessarily denigrate some of the Companions of the Prophet, mainly those who recognized Abu Bakr, 'Umar and 'Uthman above 'Ali. Ahmad considers that ahl al-sunnah wa-al-jama'ah were the true party (shi'ah) of the Prophet's family, since in his view 'Ali also thought himself below Abu Bakr, 'Umar, and 'Uthman.

The last theological party Ahmad comdems are the Khawarij, (IAY, 1:33–4). According to Ahmad, they combine the
errors of the Qadariyah (denying predestination), the Murji'ah
(over-confidence that God accepts their own faith), the Jahmiyah (disbelieving in the Basin and other things), and the Rafidah
(insulting most of the Companions). A number of their offenses
were aberrant rules of law: they thought it lawful to pray late,
to begin fasting before they saw the new moon of Ramadan, for
a woman to give herself in marriage without the intervention
of a male guardian, and other enormities.

Ahmad goes on to name the Shu'ubiyah, who held that Arabs
had no claims above non-Arabs (IAY, 1:34–5). This is usually
seen as a literary movement, but Ahmad thought it a dangerous innovation at the level of orthodox belief, as well. Ahmad's
younger contemporary, Ibn Qutaybah, wrote a book, explaining difficult passages of the Qur'an, directed against people
who said that the Qur'an was incoherent, self-contradictory,
mean, and otherwise offensive to refined literary taste. Ahmad
may have attributed such views to the Shu'ubiyah, who were
famed for their excessive pride in Persian literature. The last
group he condemns, the *ashab al-ra'y*, meaning the adherents
of opinion, are usually seen as a school of law (IAY, 1:35). They
recognize Abu Hanifah as their leader, preferring his position
to that of what the Prophet and his Companions said.

Even in a list of things to be believed, Ahmad could not stay
away from the law and other issues not obviously theological.
Strictly, theological offenses turn up in all of Ahmad's creeds,
not just some: those of the Murji'ah, Qadariyah, Shi'ah and
the so-called Jahmiyah. His wandering off into legal and social
questions shows us several things: these are an individual's
creeds, not a synod's; this individual could sound like a crank;
and yet this was the man who defined orthodoxy for a century

or more, which shows how marginal and undisciplined theology was for the Sunni party.

POLITICS

For Ahmad, politics was largely about recognizing the legitimate ruler (the imam). He did not expect to participate in decision-making. The Qur'an repeatedly enjoins Believers to obey God *and his messenger*, equating loyalty to the worldly leader with loyalty to God. Civil wars in the Islamic state nearly always had religious overtones, as each party fought for its candidate for the imamate: 'Ali against the Umayyads, Khawarij against 'Ali, Zubayrids against Umayyads, and so on. For the Shi'ah, the community that saves has usually been defined primarily defined by its loyalty to one leader – one ruler, or at least the one who ought to have been sole ruler. This stress on a personal leader is an authentically early element of Islam.

Leadership is not so prominent in Ahmad's creeds. Sunnism was largely independent of ruler: the community was meant to unite around one scheme of law and belief. Most of Ahmad's creeds mention that the ruler, whether righteous or reprobate, should be obeyed but only one mentions that he should be of the Prophet's tribe (with the Shi'ah but against the Khawarij and others; IAY, 1:26).

Ahmad was much more eager to affirm his loyalty to the earliest caliphs, presumably as part of the project of re-orienting Sunni loyalty away from particular, disappointing, rulers of the present. All of Ahmad's creeds address the succession to the Prophet, although not consistently. The Prophet died without clearly designating who should succeed him as leader. In his final illness, we are told, he appointed his elderly father-in-law, Abu Bakr, as prayer-leader (*imam*) in his place: this has been taken by Sunni Muslims to indicate he meant Abu Bakr to be the first caliph (the Arabic *khalifah* means "deputy" or "successor"). We are told of a speech he made at Ghadir Khumm not long before his death: "Of whomever I am the *mawla*, 'Ali also is his *mawla*." *Mawla* probably means "patron" or "master," and the Shi'ah take this story to indicate that Muhammad appointed 'Ali his successor. However, the story is in Ahmad's *Musnad,* as well as other Sunni sources, so the Sunni party must have interpreted it differently – probably (as others admittedly explained more clearly than Ahmad) as a successful attempt to quash complaints about 'Ali's distribution of booty but not to appoint him his successor.

Sources of all tendencies agree that some of the Companions wanted 'Ali to succeed Muhammad but 'Umar managed to get Abu Bakr acclaimed first. He lived for just two more years, then 'Umar succeeded him. A committee appointed 'Uthman as successor to 'Umar. When 'Uthman was assassinated by fellow Muslims angered by his nepotism, the First Civil War began. One party of Medinans, including those who had fought 'Uthman, immediately acclaimed 'Ali; others, notably Talhah, al-Zubayr and the Prophet's widow 'A'ishah, fought him, although they had not defended 'Uthman. Talhah and al-Zubayr were killed and 'A'ishah taken prisoner. 'Ali was also fought by a party from Syria, led by Mu'awiyah, claiming revenge for 'Uthman their kinsman. The First Civil War ended when 'Ali was killed by a Khariji and Mu'awiyah was almost universally acclaimed as caliph.

The classical Sunni view of the caliphate, which has dominated modern histories, holds that Abu Bakr, 'Umar, 'Uthman, and 'Ali were the four Rightly-Guided Caliphs (*al-khulafa' al-rashidun*), after whom came the Umayyad dynasty, founded by Mu'awiyah. A clear sign of ideology at work is the way this list fails to count 'Uthman as an Umayyad when he was

just as Umayyad as Mu'awiyah (they were both great-grand-
sons of Umayyah, as was 'Abd al-Malik, who re-established
the Umayyad dynasty after the Second Civil War). There is a
fair amount of evidence that the Umayyad caliphs and their
supporters thought the early sequence of caliphs was Abu
Bakr, 'Umar, 'Uthman, Mu'awiyah, and so on. The classical
Sunni view was not standard in Ahmad's time. He strenuously asserted that 'Ali was the fourth caliph, not against the
Shi'ah, who were inclined to put 'Ali earlier, but against fellow
self-styled adherents of the *sunnah*, who were inclined not to
recognize him as a caliph at all.

As for who were the best of the Companions (*tafdil*), it was
a separate question for Ahmad and his immediate followers
whether to style 'Ali the fourth. Ahmad was cautious on this
question. To say that 'Ali was fourth best was to put him above
Talhah, al-Zubayr, and Mu'awiyah and thus perhaps to imply
that they had been wrong to fight him. Given the Sunni insistence (against the Shi'ah) that no evil should be spoken of the
Companions, this was an uncomfortable implication to accept.
In Creeds I, II and V, Ahmad states that 'Ali was fourth caliph
and fourth best, although in Creed I he notes that some would
not say 'Ali was fourth best. In Creeds III and IV, he keeps 'Ali
equal with Talhah, al-Zubayr and the other members of the
council and in Creed VI says that after the death of 'Uthman
there was no one better than 'Ali, leaving open the possibility
that Talhah, al-Zubayr, and others were equally good.

The *masa'il* collections are likewise inconsistent. According to Salih and 'Abd Allah, Ahmad specifies Abu Bakr, 'Umar,
'Uthman, and 'Ali as regards the caliphate and Abu Bakr, 'Umar,
and 'Uthman as regards who was best (Salih, no. 349; 'Al.,
440). Abu Dawud and Ibn Hani' report that Ahmad specified
Abu Bakr, 'Umar, 'Uthman, and 'Ali, in that order, as caliphs
and the first three as the best, "but we do not rebuke whoever

makes 'Ali the fourth" (AD, 277; Ibn Hani', 2:169, but also
Sunnah, 206 *235*). Al-Khallal (died 311/923) collected and
synthesized almost all the available accounts of Ahmad's doctrine. He reports, from several sources, that Ahmad said the
best, in order, were Abu Bakr, 'Umar, 'Uthman, and 'Ali but
asserts that by most accounts (*al-mashhur*), he named only the
first three (Khallal, 2:404–10). Possibly, Ahmad himself went
back and forth on this point. Khallal also related the opinion
of Sa'sa'ah ibn Suhan, an early Kufan Follower, that Abu Bakr
and 'Umar had been appointed to the caliphate by God and
'Uthman by the people, apparently an attempt to lessen the
responsibility of choosing between him and 'Ali (*Sunnah*, 194
223). The Hanbali school after Khallal remained divided.

At one extreme of the spectrum of opinion in Ahmad's
time were those who recognized Mu'awiyah as the fourth
caliph and preferred him to 'Ali. They were sometimes called
the Nasibah (though not by Ahmad). The Nasibah ("hostiles")
were increasingly restricted to Syria in the ninth century and
disappeared during the tenth. Slightly further along were those
who recognized Abu Bakr, 'Umar, and 'Uthman as the best of
the Companions, in that order, but did not distinguish 'Ali
from the rest. Khallal called this position the *mashhur*. One
ninth-century writer on heresies expressly says that Ahmad
espoused this view, as did his fellow Baghdadi traditionists
Yahya ibn Ma'in (died 233/848) and Abu Khaythamah (died
234/849; *Imamah*, 66).

Further along the spectrum were those with whom Ahmad
sometimes seems to have identified himself, who held that Abu
Bakr, 'Umar, 'Uthman, and 'Ali were both the first four caliphs
and, in that order, the four best Companions. This became the
classical Sunni view in the tenth century. The same writer on
heresies identifies this as the position of several Basrans from
the generation before Ahmad, notably his shaykhs Yahya ibn

Sa'id al-Qattan (died 198/813) and 'Abd al-Rahman ibn Mahdi (died 198/814).

Next came those who would not choose between 'Ali and 'Uthman (an unacceptable position to Ahmad, for it implied that the Companions may have erred in naming 'Uthman first). The Medinan jurisprudent Malik (died 179/795) is sometimes said to have taken this position, as is Ahmad's shaykh Yazid ibn Harun (died 206/821–2; KMT 2:806; 'Ilal 3:473 2:272). Ahmad's Yemeni shaykh 'Abd al-Razzaq was sometimes classified with this group and sometimes further along the spectrum, among those who positively preferred 'Ali to 'Uthman (KMT 2:806; Lisan 3:433). A modest preference for 'Ali was especially popular in Kufa, as was Shi'ism generally. Among others, the traditionist and Qur'anic reciter al-A'mash (died 148/765?) and the jurisprudent Abu Hanifah (died 150/767) were said to prefer 'Ali to 'Uthman. However, this preference was not restricted to Kufans: among others the prominent Basran traditionist, Shu'bah (died 160/776), was also said to espouse it (Lisan 3:433).

Sunni hadith critics commonly distinguished between tashayyu', a mild sort of Shi'ism that accepted the rights of Abu Bakr and 'Umar to the caliphate, only preferring 'Ali to 'Uthman, and rafd, (rejection), the extreme position of preferring 'Ali even to Abu Bakr and 'Umar. The Zaydiyah, for a very long time the predominant Shi'ah in Yemen, are usually identified as accepting Abu Bakr and 'Umar. Ahmad related that their imam, Zayd ibn 'Ali, declared that Abu Bakr and 'Umar were righteous leaders, although he counted the Zaydiyah after as adherents of rafd on account of their espousing of active rebellion (Sunnah, 197 226; IAY, 1:33).

Many Mu'tazilah took the position that, although 'Ali might have been the best, Abu Bakr and 'Umar were none the less, good enough to be legitimate caliphs. The Isma'iliyah and the

Twelver Shi'ah (also called the Imamiyah) held the extreme position that 'Ali should have been the Prophet's immediate successor and thus that Abu Bakr and 'Umar were usurpers.

AHMAD THE FUNDAMENTALIST?

In some ways, Ahmad is reminiscent of American Protestant Fundamentalists of the early twentieth century. These Fundamentalists were named for the half-dozen "fundamentals" of the Christian faith they identified: commonly, biblical inerrancy, creation in six days, the Virgin Birth, the sacrificial atonement, the Second Coming, and the resurrection of the body. It is a very Protestant list: a Catholic list would include the Sacraments (admittedly, their omission avoids controversy between adult- and infant-baptizing Protestants). It is a list of propositions to be believed and is not concerned with ethics. It is almost wholly concerned with biblical literalism, which is one reason some object to applying the term "fundamentalist" to the militant Muslim reactionaries of the later twentieth century: literalism is not an issue for them; their concerns are public decorum, equality of Muslims and non-Muslims, and other largely ethical issues. "Fundamentalist" probably comes to mind because, like American Protestants, modern Muslim reactionaries are associated with defensiveness and intolerance.

Ahmad's creed may be considered Fundamentalist for its basing the division between those who are in and those who are out mainly what on they believe, not what they do. Khariji Islam was fully orthopractic: it defined Muslims by whether they followed the law and declared cardinal sinners to have apostatized. Sunni Muslims held to a strictly non-ethical definition of unbelief. "Do not call any of them an unbeliever on account of a sin."

Ahmad's creed is also Fundamentalist in its defensiveness
and intolerance. It is a series more of rejections than positive
affirmations of what he rejoices to be assured of. His insistence on what has come down from past authority, however
repugnant to reason or taste ("Even if the ears are repelled by
it and the hearer disgusted, he must believe in it" – Creed III,
IAY 1:242), may easily remind one of a Christian Fundamentalist insisting on the Creation or the Virgin Birth. However,
Fundamentalists have never expressed themselves in such
resolute opposition to reason as Ahmad. On the contrary, they
have proposed some very elaborate rationalistic defences of
their Fundamentals, notably Creation Science. In the manner
of would-be Sunni theologians, whom Ahmad despised, they
have thought that reason should arrive at the same ends as their
dogmatic assertions from revelation.

Fundamentalists have defended the authority of the Bible,
whereas Ahmad never defended the authority of the Qur'an,
but this is because he had no need to: the Khawarij, Mu'tazilah,
and the rest of Ahmad's adversaries denigrated hadith, not
the Qur'an. However, Ahmad's treatment of hadith is not
very like the Fundamentalists' treatment of the Bible. Against
Roman Catholics and critical scholars, the Fundamentalists
emphatically elevate the Bible above the level of tradition. In
contrast, Ahmad likes tradition. He is not trying to get behind
tradition to original revelation, as the Protestant Reformers
did, to varying degrees (and as many modern Muslims, liberals
and reactionaries alike, do): his concern is to exclude recent
innovations. Protestant Fundamentalism has no analogy to
the authority of the Companions, which Ahmad emphatically
affirms. (Admittedly, although they have ignored the early
church's interpretations of Scripture, Fundamentalists have
insistently followed its ascriptions of various books to Apos-
tles.) Whereas al-Shafi'i presses a Protestant-style distinction

between revelation (the Qur'an and the prophetic hadith) and tradition (the dicta of Companions and others), Ahmad is at most working his way towards disengaging the Prophet from early Muslim society, by distinguishing sharply between his example and that of his Companions.

Fundamentalism has sometimes been defined by the simplification of a traditional symbol system. Ibn Kathir, a Shafi'i writer of the Mamluk period (died 774/1373), has been identified as a Fundamentalist for his sweeping away of the long tradition of respecting multiple interpretations of the Qur'an in favor of one correct interpretation for each verse (Calder). His Qur'anic commentary has emerged as the favorite of today's Muslim reactionaries, at least among Sunnis. (It has recently become the first extensive medieval commentary translated into English, although abridged.) This clearly shows where Ahmad is not a Fundamentalist: he does not simplify. He resists theological sophistication but in an argument with his contemporaries, not an attempt to repudiate a long theological tradition. Regarding hadith and the law, he never cuts them down to manageable proportions but respects the immensity of the tradition in all its complexity.

Ahmad's hesitancy in giving juridical opinions also has an un-Fundamentalist feel. We live in a rational age. Capitalism has the cultural tendency to direct our attention to what is calculable (such as the market demand for such and such a commodity) and away from what is not (such as what is in good taste). Fundamentalist simplification moves in the same rationalizing direction: just as there is always one unambiguous answer in book-keeping, so there should be in religion. The Islamic tradition identifies a range of correct answers: multiple orthodox readings of the words of the Qur'an, multiple orthodox interpretations, multiple opinions from Companions and Followers, multiple schools of law, multiple disagreements within each school and more. This is definitely not the wide-open pluralism expected by the Western liberal tradition but neither does it provide an Islamic law for reactionaries to apply, like a Muslim version of the Code Napoléon. The fourteenth-century Hanbali, Ibn Taymiyah, is a favorite author among modern Muslim reactionaries, but their interest in Ahmad is insufficient to keep his *masa'il* in print.

SUNNI THEOLOGY AFTER AHMAD

Ahmad's opposition to theological speculation was somewhat more successful than his opposition to writing down the opinions of jurisprudents, including his own. Two centuries later, there was rioting in Baghdad when a Shafi'i preacher from Khurasan tried to expound Ash'ari theology in a mosque. Philosophy, in as much as it proposed to construct entirely rational systems, independent of revelation, largely disappeared from the Sunni world after the twelfth century. (It lived longer in a Shi'i context.) The chief civilian notables of the later Middle Ages, when political power was held mainly by Turkish soldiers, were professors of law. For example, when Tamerlane appeared before a city, it was typically judges and professors of law who turned out to treat with him.

However, Ahmad's vehement opposition to would-be Sunni theology was not ultimately successful. Ahmad could not stay entirely away from theological disputation; for example, he seems to have made a collection of Qur'anic verses to refute the Jahmi doctrine that the Qur'an was created (*Sunnah*, 169–77 *192–206*). In the next century, a follower composed a refutation of the Jahmiyah in the style of *kalam* and attributed it to Ahmad (*Radd* and *Siyar* 11:286–7). Just as King Cnut could not stop the tide, so Ahmad could not keep Muslim intellectuals from complicating doctrine. As late as the fourteenth century, there were debates between Ash'ari theologians and traditionalist opponents but the game had largely been lost and even the Hanbali school was largely Ash'ari in its theology; for example, the old insistence on the non-created nature of the pronunciation of the Qur'an was given up. Even in theology, Ahmad's prescription would not last.

5

PIETY

As a jurisprudent, Ahmad was chiefly concerned with what the revealed law required and what it forbade. However, it is often difficult to tell from his terminology whether a particular activity is forbidden outright or simply discouraged; his concern with law quickly shaded off into his concern with the things a sincere believer does over and above the minimum required. Next to the *Musnad*, Ahmad's greatest literary monument is *al-Zuhd*, a collection of renunciant sayings of the prophets (mostly, but not only, Muhammad), Muhammad's Companions, and his Followers in the next generation. Ahmad lived a notably austere life, from which he derived much of his authority.

The most famous Muslim renunciants of the past thousand years are the Sufis. From around 1100 to around 1900, Sufism was a crucial element of mainstream Islam, the great connector of disparate intellectual disciplines, community feeling, and personal piety. Recently, Sufism has been widely repudiated by educated Muslims, such as most of the Salafis, who associate it with weakness *vis à vis* European colonialism, superstition, tricks, and moral and theological laxity. More subtly, there seem to be too many urgent tasks for Muslims to do in this world for them to occupy their free time with devotional exercises to improve their standing in the next. As with the scholasticism of the law, Ahmad in some ways anticipates the modern unease with Sufism; however, his main expressed worry was not that the renunciants of his time failed to meet the highest moral standard but that they set a standard too high for the great majority, spoiling the unity and equality of the community.

AHMAD AND THE RENUNCIANT TRADITION

The early renunciant tradition, as depicted by Ahmad and others, was primarily about a reorientation from this world to the next. It was based on an interpretation of the Qur'an as calling for such a reorientation, which is, I think, a credible reading. Here are some verses I happen to have been shown in another connection:

> And give the kinsman his right, and the needy and the traveller; and never squander; the squanderers are brothers of Satan, and Satan is unthankful to his Lord. But if thou turnest from them, seeking mercy from thy Lord that thou hopest for, then speak unto them gentle words. And keep not thy hand chained to thy neck, nor outspread it widespread altogether, or thou wilt sit reproached and denuded. Surely the Lord outspreads and straitens His provision unto whom He will; surely He is aware of and sees His servants.
>
> (Q. 17:26–30, Arberry translation)

Biblical expositions of the law also sometimes depart from the rules to the larger theological framework:

> Six days shalt thou labour and do all thy work: but the seventh day is the Sabbath of the LORD thy God …: for in six days the LORD made heaven and earth, the sea, and all that in them is, and rested the seventh day: wherefore the LORD blessed the Sabbath day, and hallowed it.
>
> (Ex. 20:9–11, KJV).

The Qur'an veers even more insistently into the larger context of God's direction of all things and the cosmic choice with which He confronts us: whether to be heedful or not. Muslims today do not seem more dour than other people. Christians are likely to find them remarkably (dangerously) confident of their standing with God. "Surely he is aware of and sees his servants" they take as comfort, not constant threat. Presumably, many eighth-century Muslims likewise felt comforted. However, the early renunciants were of a very different mind. Ahmad documented their response to the Qur'an in his collection on renunciation. Modern scholars may doubt whether he was accurately informed, especially about the earliest renunciants, but this was the pattern after which he tried to live his own life, so the important thing for now is that this was his perception of how the early generations had lived.

To the early renunciants, the Qur'an was frightening. The Prophet's Companion, Ibn 'Umar, on reciting a verse of the Qur'an, wept until he collapsed (*Zuhd*, 192 *240*). The Prophet's favorite wife 'A'ishah, hearing the Qur'an, wept until her veil was soaked (*Zuhd*, 164 *205*). The Basran, Malik ibn Dinar (died 130/747–8?), hearing the Qur'anic verse: "If this Qur'an were sent down on a mountain, you would see it humbled and cloven from fear of God," wept and said, "I swear to you, no servant believes in this Qur'an without his heart's splitting" (*Zuhd*, 319 *386*).

Death was frightening, since after it came the Last Judgment and the sight of God. The eight-century Basran, Mu'adhah al-'Adawiyah, slept neither by day nor night, fearing that each would be her last, and wore thin clothes so that the cold would keep her awake (*Zuhd*, 208 *257*). The Basran, Mutarrif ibn al-Shikhkhir (died 95/713–14), said:

> If I were poised between Paradise and Hell, then a voice cried to me "O Mutarrif, would you like us to tell you in which of

them you are to be?" I should prefer to be cold ashes to being told in which of them I was to be.

(*Zuhd*, 241 *295*; variant at 238 *292*).

Abu 'Ubaydah ibn al-Jarrah (died 18/639–40), one of the nine Companions promised Paradise, wished he had been a ram slaughtered by his family and eaten (*Zuhd*, 184 *230*; also attributed to another Companion, 204 *253*). The Kufan Companion Ibn Mas'ud (died 32/652–3?) would have preferred not to be raised after death (*Zuhd*, 156 *195*).

Yet it was as well to think on one's death, for that would reduce one's attachment to this world. The early eighth-century Kufan, al-Rabi' ibn Abi Rashid, refused a friend's invitation to sit down, lest it corrupt his heart to cease recollecting death (*Zuhd*, 395 *472*), and Raja' ibn Haywah, a Palestinian jurisprudent (died 112/730–1), said, "No man increases his recollection of death without abandoning joy (*farah*) and envy" (*Zuhd*, 390 *466*). He would have recommended abandoning joy in as much as it was for anything worldly – anything short of one's salvation at the Last Judgment. The Basran, al-'Ala' ibn Ziyad (died 94/712–13), suggested people should imagine themselves on the point of death, which would conduce to obeying God (*Zuhd*, 255 *312*).

The early renunciants favored reorientation from this world to the next, and so put a low value on worldly activities, such as social service, and a high value on ritual observance. Abu al-Darda' (died 30s/650s) declared that he would rather say *Allahu akbar* a hundred times than give away a hundred dinars in charity (*Zuhd*, 137 *170*; attributed to someone else, 393 *470*). 'Abd al-Rahman ibn al-Aswad (died 99/717–18), who was just skin and bone, made 700 sets of bowings (*rak'ahs*) per day (*Zuhd*, 360 *430*). Men were commended for being imperturbable when at prayer. When Ibn Mas'ud prostrated himself, "he was like a garment thrown down" (*Zuhd*, 158 *197*). The same was said of the Kufan, al-Rabi' ibn Khuthaym (died 63/682–3?), with the added detail that sparrows could alight on him (*Zuhd*, 341 *410*; said of another Companion, 359 *429*). 'Abd Allah ibn al-Zubayr (died 73/693), as he stood in prayer, failed to be distracted by a missile that tore away part of his garment (*Zuhd*, 200 *249*).

Qur'an recitation was a prominent part of renunciant devotions, as well as ritual prayer. The Kufan, Sa'id ibn Jubayr (died 95/713–14), recited the whole Qur'an every two nights (*Zuhd*, 370 *443*) while the Basran Thabit al-Bunani (died 120s/738–48) recited it daily (*Hilyah* 2:321, quoting Ahmad). Some renunciants integrated extensive recitation with normal rituals; for example, al-Rabi' ibn Khuthaym would recite one verse all night, inclining and prostrating himself (*Zuhd*, 336 *405*). Supererogatory fasting was a common devotional form; the Basran, Ibn Sirin (died 110/729), fasted on alternate days, never becoming accustomed to either one regime or the other (*Zuhd*, 307 *373*). Renunciants continually engaged in *dhikr* (recollection), the repetition of pious phrases either alone or in a group in the mosque. Al-Hasan al-Basri recalled how the pious predecessors had preferred to be in a state of ritual purity when they recollected God, which indicates a formal litany (*Zuhd*, 258 *315*). His Basran contemporary, Khulayd al-'Asri, would make the dawn prayer, then recollect God at the mosque until the sun was fully up, then go home, lock the door, and repeat pious phrases until he was either overcome by sleep or it was time for the noon prayer (*Zuhd*, 237 *290–1*).

Private devotions were best, for privacy ensured that they were performed to honor God, not to attract compliments from men. The Basran, 'Amir ibn 'Abd Qays (died 55/674–5?), was annoyed if anyone saw him praying (*Zuhd*, 223 *273–4*). The Syrian Makhul (died 110s/729–38) declared, "There are two eyes that will not be touched by Hellfire: an eye that has wept for fear of God and an eye that has kept vigil out of the Muslims' sight" (*Zuhd*, 386 463). The Kufan, Ibrahim al-Nakha'i (died 96/714–15?), covered the copy of the Qur'an from which he was reading whenever a visitor came (*Zuhd*, 364–5 437).

Early renunciants paid as little attention as they could to living comfortably. The Syrian Abu Idris al-Khawlani (died 80/699–700) said, "Whoever makes God his sole concern will have sufficient to concern him. Whoever finds a concern in every valley, God will not care in which he perishes" (*Zuhd*, 380 456). Tawus, a famous Yemeni (died 106/724–5?), prayed to be deprived of children and wealth (*Zuhd*, 375 449). The Kufan, Masruq (died 63/682–3?), said, "I am never more trusting of my provision than when the servant says 'We haven't a *qafis* (a measure of dry goods, meaning here grain) or a dirham'" (*Zuhd*, 349 419).

AN IDEAL WITHIN THE RANGE OF MOST MEN

Ahmad's collection *al-Zuhd* (assembled, with many additions, by his son 'Abd Allah though the citations above are all for items related by Ahmad) has almost nothing later than the early eighth century, although we know from other sources that Ahmad was interested in later figures as well; for example, he is the source for the remark of Ibrahim ibn Adham (died 163/779–80) that God will not consider a saint anyone who loves desire (*Hilyah* 8:19–20). Most of the attitudes and practices of the earliest renunciants were still to be found among their successors in the later eighth century and after. Ahmad's shaykh Yahya ibn Sa'id al-Qattan would faint on hearing the Qur'an recited (*Amr*, 116). Exaggerated fear of death and judgment is more difficult to find but Yahya ibn Mu'adh al-Razi (died 258/872), for example, recommended in rhyme that one make death the subject of one's thought (*Hilyah* 10:58). Supererogatory ritual observance continued to be a commonplace of renunciant life; for example, the Baghdadi, Ma'ruf al-Karkhi (died around 200/815–16), in whose circle Ahmad sometimes sat, would fast unless someone invited him to eat (*TB* 13:202–3). And other forms of austerity continued to be found. For example, when Ahmad called on Shu'ayb ibn Harb (died 197/812–13?) in the company of Abu Khaythamah, Shu'ayb noticed that Abu Khaythamah's sleeves were luxuriously long and called for a knife to cut them short, for "Who writes hadith with long sleeves?" They left without hearing any hadith, although Ahmad later took dictation from Shu'ayb in Mecca (*TB* 9:241).

Renunciation naturally changed with time and began to be more formal. From about the early ninth century, masters and disciples begin to be identified. Some masters had huge retinues; for example, 120 are said to have gathered around Abu Turab al-Nakhshabi (died 245/859–60; *Hilyah* 10:48). Technical terms begin to appear; Ahmad's Syrian contemporary Mansur ibn 'Ammar declared:

> Be he praised who made the hearts of the knowers containers of recollection, the hearts of the worldlings containers of desire, the hearts of the renunciants containers of utter dependence, the hearts of the needy containers of contentment and the hearts of the utterly dependent containers of satisfaction.

(*Hilyah* 9:327).

The word used for "knowers" ('*arifin*) suggests direct apprehension and mystical experience. "Utter dependence" translates *tawakkul*, a Qur'anic word that ninth-century renunciants applied to extreme feats of austerity. Someone asked the Sufi Ibn al-Jalla' (died 306/918), "What about those who go into the desert without provision or supplies, claiming that they are practising *tawakkul*, and so die?" Ibn al-Jalla' said, "They are the men of truth. If they die, the wergild is charged to the killer" (*TB* 5:215). In other words, blame God if you dare. The recorded sermons of people like al-Hasan al-Basri seem to be directed at all Muslims but people like Mansur ibn 'Ammar seem to be using a special vocabulary to address specialists in renunciation.

The new Sunni party that emerged in Ahmad's youth was hostile mainly to rationalists in law and theology; however, they were also uneasy with contemporary renunciant teaching and practice. Ahmad's shaykh Ibn 'Uyaynah (died Mecca, 198/814?) is described and quoted in much the same way as numerous earlier renunciants; for example, he endorsed the contemplation of death and said a learned man (*'alim*) was not he who knew good and evil but who actively pursued good and eschewed evil, and personally ate plain barley bread (rather than wheat) for forty or sixty years (*Hilyah* 7:273, 274, 299). On the other hand, he is sometimes quoted as opposing outward humility itself:

> Renunciation (*zuhd*) concerns what God has forbidden. As for what God has pronounced licit, God has made it a matter of indifference for you. The prophets married, rode, and ate but when God forbade them something, they accepted his forbidding and thus were renunciant with regard to it.

(*Hilyah* 7:297)

Numerous early renunciants had called for inward humility to match outward, but the limitation of outward renunciation to no more than that from which everyone was asked to abstain is new.

The church went through similar changes centuries earlier. Before Constantine, when the Christians were a small, persecuted sect, it was natural for zealots to dominate. Who was in and who out? Those who had faith were in, of course, but how could it be known who had faith? Those who followed the rules had faith. However, during the fourth century, when Christianity became the expected religious affiliation of all Roman citizens, the Church filled up with people who were not particularly zealous. It would have been quite impractical for the church henceforth to demand an exceptionally high level of morality. Those who demanded zealotry were excluded as sectaries (notably the Donatists in North Africa). Now who was in and who out? Those who had faith were still in but now that meant those who professed orthodox beliefs. What was in it now for the zealots? The Donatists' great enemy, Augustin of Hippo (died 430), can be read as supplying a new inward piety for the zealots, with a strong emphasis on Original Sin and personal depravity. They were to work on themselves (perhaps in combination, later, with monasticism) rather than worry about the lax majority.

Renunciants such as al-Hasan al-Basri lived when the Muslims were a small sect, or at least a tiny élite living atop a great mass of tribute-paying non-Muslims. Descriptions of his and other pious Muslims' poverty sit next to casual references to pensions (tribute received by veterans of the Islamic conquests) and servants. For example, al-Hasan would invite all his visitors to eat, one group after another. When the slave girl announced that they had nothing left, he bade her bring some barley gruel (*Zuhd*, 265–6 *325*). His contempt for trading suggests the outlook of a rentier class. "There is no good in the people of the market. I have heard that one of them will do his brother out of a dirham" (*Zuhd*, 288 *351*). Such features survived into Ahmad's lifetime and explain some of the similarity between his and his teachers' piety and that of the early renunciants. For example, in the story mentioned above of Shu'ayb objecting to long sleeves, he calls for a slave (*ghulam*) to bring him the knife. Ahmad lived mainly off rents. According to his son 'Abd Allah, "Nobody saw him except in the mosque, attending a funeral, or visiting a sick person. He disliked to walk in the markets" (*Hilyah* 9:184).

However, when most people were Muslims, at least in places like Baghdad, it was futile to expect that most should spend their time in religious exercises or fighting the holy war, relying on servants and tribute from non-Muslims. Like medieval Christians, the Sunni community eventually achieved a majoritarian piety by defining membership strictly in terms of the profession of orthodox beliefs, not necessarily living up to them. As Ahmad says, "Do not call any of them an unbeliever on account of a sin" (IAY, 1:27). Like medieval Christians with regard to monastic orders, the Sunni community came to recognize special institutions, in their case the Sufi orders, to accommodate those zealots not content with an average level of piety.

There was also a religious reason for Ibn 'Uyaynah's call to follow the normal rules and no more. Piety runs a spectrum, from moralistic religion to mysticism. Moralistic religion ("ascetical" and "theocratic" are other words that scholars have applied) is about obeying a transcendent God, whereas mystical religion is about communion with an immanent God. Different religious forms are located at different points on the spectrum; for example, Calvinism is moralistic relative to Lutheranism and Eastern Orthodox Christianity mystical relative to Roman Catholic. Early Sunni piety looks highly moralistic. Moral demands are necessarily the same for everyone, in every place, at every time. For example, adultery is not sometimes forbidden and sometimes allowed but always forbidden; supporting one's family is not sometimes required and sometimes not but always required. If a person did something not everyone might do, such as staying up every night to recite the Qur'an, it was evidently not in response to a moral demand from God. To moralists, this looked dangerously like a stunt: "Look what I can do." (To be fair, someone like Thabit al-Bunani would almost surely have said he recited the whole Qur'an daily as an act of obedience.) There was bound to be tension between the ever more thoroughgoing moralists and the emerging Muslim mystics.

AHMAD'S PRACTICE

Ahmad has been seen as advocating a doctrine like Ibn 'Uyaynah's, in which extravagant austerity was not required and indeed specifically discouraged. The foremost advocate of this view is an Israeli scholar, Nimrod Hurvitz, who characterizes Ahmad's program as "mild asceticism." Hurvitz cites evidence such as this disciple's recollection of how Ahmad dressed:

> I do not know that I have seen anyone whose clothes were cleaner or who took better care of himself as to his moustaches, the hair of his head, and the hair of his body, nor whose clothes were cleaner or whiter than Ahmad ibn Hanbal. His clothes were in between. His outer wrap was worth fifteen dirhams, while his shirt underneath could be bought for about a dinar. It had neither reprehensible delicacy nor disreputable roughness.

(*Siyar* 11:208)

There is a case to be made that Ahmad advocated a moderate style of life – a Sunni style of renunciation, compatible with rearing a family and pursuing a trade; a style less strenuous than that of early renunciants such as al-Hasan al-Basri and Malik ibn Dinar or contemporaries such as Bishr ibn al-Harith. Whatever his own avoidance of it, he is said to have commanded his own sons to frequent the market (*Wara'*, 22 17). When consulted about someone who proposed to withdraw from society and stay at home, Ahmad objected that this might lead to something wrong, mainly "That he should expect to be sent something [as alms]. If he went out and practiced a craft, that would be preferable to me" (*Wara'*, 24 20). When told of another's plan to go into the desert without provision or supplies, he became angry and said:

> *Uff uff* nooo nooo (*la la madda biha sawtah*) – unless with provision, companions and a caravan (*Hathth*, 137) .... I have not heard of any of the Companions of the Messenger of God or the Followers who did that (*Hathth*, 140) .... It is proper for all persons to depend on God (*yatawakkaluna 'ala Allah*) but they should depend on themselves for gain (*Hathth*, 156).

In particular, they should not be a burden to other Muslims. "*Tawakkul* is good; however, a man must not be a charge on others. He should work, in order to make himself and his family independent" (*Hathth*, 158).

Ahmad was critical of celibacy, declaring: "Celibacy has nothing to do with Islam .... The Prophet married fourteen women and left nine widows. If Bishr ibn al-Harith had married, his whole life would have been perfect" (*Wara'*, 94 *118*). It was reported to Ahmad that someone had said, "Ahmad ibn Hanbal and Bishr ibn al-Harith are not, in my opinion, renunciants (*zuhhad*). Ahmad has bread that he eats while Bishr has dirhams coming to him from Khurasan." Ahmad smiled and said, "Is he a renunciant?" (*Wara'*, 138 *187*). Ahmad stood for a wider definition of renunciant than did others (and perhaps suspected that some were preaching a more severe renunciation than they actually practiced).

Ahmad did not have particularly close relations with contemporary renunciants. He probably met the Baghdadi, Ma'ruf al-Karkhi (IAY, 1:381). However, he apparently quoted nothing from him in *al-Zuhd*. Abu Hamzah al-Baghdadi (died 269/882–3?) was an important figure who would sit in Ahmad's circle;

Ahmad would ask him, "What do you say about it, Sufi?" (IAY, 1:268). This shows that Ahmad knew the term "Sufi" and applied it to an early mystic. His question sounds ironic, although his biographer indicates that Abu Hamzah repeated the story with pride. The story does not indicate any long-term engagement between them; for all we know, Ahmad saw Abu Hamzah only once and recognized him as a renunciant by his dress.

Ahmad disparaged some of the principal renunciant practices of the ninth century, such as roaming from place to place: "*Siyaha* has nothing to do with Islam" (Ibn Hani', 2:176). When someone told him of a group that met to pray, recite the Qur'an, and recollect God (that is, repeatedly recite short praises). Ahmad responded that it was enough to read from the bound copy, recollect God to oneself, and to seek hadith. Meeting in public for these purposes was an innovation to be condemned (IAY, 1:255). From the earliest literature of Sufi doctrine it appears that their main activity in the century or so after Ahmad's death was to sit about trading definitions of technical terms such as "knowledge" and "dependence": Ahmad would have considered such meetings a sheer waste of time. The only reason to meet in public was to trade hadith – otherwise people should stick to devotions in the privacy of their own homes.

However, I am inclined to think that Ahmad was in two minds about renunciation. His personal practice was austere by comparison with that of his friends and neighbors (and certainly of the author and expected readers of this book). He fasted every Monday and Thursday (traditional Jewish fast days, but the Prophet's example was what mattered to Ahmad), on the three "days of whiteness" before the full moon, and always after returning from Samarra (*Siyar* 11:208–9, 223). According to one report, he recited a seventh of the Qur'an every day, hence the whole text weekly (*Hilyah* 9:181, 211) and, before being flogged, made 300 sets of bowings every day, 150 a day afterwards (*Hilyah* 9:181). He seems to have maintained regular night-time devotions. Once, he was appalled to find that a visitor had not used any of the water set out so he could perform his ablutions. He said, "A traditionist who hasn't a *wird* (set voluntary prayer) at night?"; his guest said, "I am traveling", but Ahmad would take no excuses: "Even if you are traveling. Masruq made the pilgrimage, and did not sleep save in prostration" (*Manaqib*, 199 *273*; for Masruq's pilgrimage, see *Zuhd*, 349 *418*).

He continually ran up against the inclinations of friends and neighbors to live less abstemiously than he thought right. His son Salih recalled having to hide anything new, to avoid his censure (*Sirah*, 41). When he came to dictate some hadith about renunciation to Salih, he found that Salih had directed his concubine to lay down a mat and a pillow for him to sit on; he had them removed and sat on the bare ground instead (*Manaqib*, 245–6 *332*). He reproached his son 'Abd Allah for having smooth feet from not walking barefoot (*TMD* 5:298).

Ahmad condemned the fashion of plastering the walls of houses (as opposed to living with the bare bricks), allowing only that the floor might be plastered, to stop dust (*Wara'*, 134 *182*). He did not himself wear renunciant clothing, at least after he had finished traveling in search of hadith, but this may have represented no more than the customary preference for keeping renunciation private. He once reproached a traditionist for not wearing renunciant clothing (*Wara'*, 128 *171*). His disciple al-Marrudhi said, "When he was at home, he usually sat cross-legged, humbly. When he was out, the severity of his humility was not apparent, as it was inside" (*Manaqib*, 209 *287*). He was sometimes found in clothes that were dirty and sweat-stained. Attending a circumcision party, "He ate until they brought some pudding (*faludhaj*), which he refused." The host pressed him, "whereupon he ate one mouthful but no more" (*Manaqib*,

252 *339*). In another version, he continued to refuse it (*Siyar* 11:219). He left another circumcision party when someone pointed out a chair with silver decorations. The host begged him to return, as did the guest of honor, their mutual teacher 'Affan – but Ahmad refused (*Sirah*, 48).

I have already mentioned Ahmad's chronic lack of cash and hand-to-mouth lifestyle. In line with the renunciant preference for the other world, he told a leading disciple, "Nothing equals poverty in merit. When your family asks you for something and you are unable to provide it, what a reward is yours" (*Manaqib*, 197 *271*). After refusing a gift of 3000 dinars, he told a son, "When I haven't one coin, then I rejoice" (*TMD* 5:305; see also Ibn Hani', 2:185). Trading and practising a craft were better than begging but it was plainly best, in his opinion, to avoid either.

He did not always and resolutely deprecate celibacy. A remembered conversation shows his ambivalence (and perhaps the wistful remembrance of youthful feats of self-denial):

> I told Abu 'Abd Allah … that the self-deniers were saying that there is nothing better than paucity and hunger and that if a man accustomed himself to not eating save every two or three days, he would be rewarded the same as someone who fasted perpetually. He said, "This is possible only for someone who is alone. As for one who has dependents, how can he be so strong? I broke my fast yesterday, and today my lower self impelled me to break it (again). There is nothing to equal poverty. I remember those young men of prayer". Then he said, "If they satisfy their appetites on bread and dates, what (more) do they want?". I asked Abu 'Abd Allah whether a man would be rewarded for suppressing appetites. He said, "And how should he not be rewarded? Ibn 'Umar said, 'I have not eaten to satiety for four months.'"

(*Wara'*, 81–2 *100*).

He was in two minds concerning the principle of *qisar al-amal*, "shortening hope." Told that Ibn 'Uyaynah had said, "Your concern for tomorrow's provision will be counted a sin," Ahmad lamented, "Who is so strong as this?" (*Wara'*, 62 *80*). This shows Ahmad, the "mild ascetic," hoping to tone down the demands of a life of piety. *Qisar al-amal* is how he himself defined renunciation to a ragged traveler who said he had come to Baghdad only to salute him (*Sirah*, 46–7). He explained the hadith *khayr al-rizq ma yakfi* (of which the *Musnad* has three versions) thus: "It is food for one day at a time: one does not concern oneself with tomorrow's provision" (*Wara'*, 101 *126*). He was also in two minds about the renunciants of the past, the spiritual athletes remembered in *al-Zuhd*. Telling stories of the *wari'in* (persons especially careful not to do anything remotely dubious), Ahmad exclaimed, "I beg God not to hate us. Where are we by comparison with them?" (*Manaqib*, 276–7 *369*).

He may have been in two minds even about spiritual concerts. On the whole, he and his followers strongly disapproved of music-making, seeing it as a frivolous distraction from performing devotions and trading hadith. Yet a shocking story circulated in Hanbali circles from about the end of the ninth century – from Ahmad's lifetime, if it is genuine. His son Salih invited an Ibn al-Khabbazah to sing renunciant poems, one night. By one account, he thought it was safe because his father had gone to bed, then heard a noise on the roof, went up to investigate, and, in his words, "saw my father on the roof, listening with his train under his armpit, prancing about on the roof as if he were dancing." According to other versions, Ahmad listened from behind a door, swaying gently. Ibn al-Jawzi, who relates the series of stories, does not deny them, although he protests that at least there was no profane singing involved and suggesting that the detail of dancing was a later, tendentious interpolation (*Talbis*, 317–18).

One might explain these contradictory reports by a struggle to define his legacy, with some followers invoking his name to justify bourgeois conformity and others to justify self-denial and social withdrawal. Then choosing the quotations that agree with one's own predilections or, more responsibly, despairs of pinning down Ahmad's actual position. I prefer to accept almost all reports, at least from the first generation of his followers. First, they come from people who knew Ahmad personally, with no such long and troubled transmission history as goes with accounts of, for example, the Companions of the Prophet. Second, no early source known to me seems systematically biased; for example, *al-Wara'*, collected by Ahmad's disciple, Abu Bakr al-Marrudhi, includes sayings of both tendencies. Ahmad's dilemma was that he admired the heroic renunciation of early Muslims and wanted to imitate it but distrusted it in contemporaries in as much as it seemed to get in the way of a moralistic, hadith-based, Islam accessible to everyone. The incoherence of his Sunnism was, to some extent, corrected about twenty-five years after his death, when al-Junayd (died 298/911?) met the moralists halfway by developing a Sufism that sounded innocuous. For example, whereas some early Sufis talked about union with God, Junayd taught that the Sufi inevitably returns after union to a state of separation; a position comforting to moralists who distrust esoterism and stress divine transcendence. In consequence, the Sunnism that became general from the tenth century onwards was able to include a place for Sufism. However, there would always be tension – such is the nature of moralism and mysticism – and modern disdain for Sufism is not a wholly unprecedented phenomenon.

As Ahmad lay on his deathbed, he was asked to name a successor. "Of whom shall we ask questions after you?" Ahmad answered, "Ask 'Abd al-Wahhab." Someone objected that he had little knowledge (of hadith). "He is a good man," said Ahmad. "One like him will be enabled to hit on the truth" (*Wara'*, 10 5). Despite Ahmad's devotion to the collection and sorting of hadith and his reputation as a perspicuous jurisprudent, he was chiefly remembered as choosing a successor for his moral qualities. When someone complained of Ma'ruf al-Karkhi that he had little religious knowledge, meaning hadith, Ahmad dismissed the criticism: "Be quiet (God protect you). Is the required knowledge anything but what Ma'ruf attained?" (*TB* 13:201). The life of piety, not scholarly expertise, was what mattered most.

CONCLUSION

Ahmad was Sunnism's leading figure in the first half of the ninth century. By the first half of the tenth century, the great majority of Muslims had come to identify themselves as adherents of the Sunnah. In this respect, his programme was a great success. Yet Ahmad himself was a melancholy figure. This was doubtless to do with his personality and individual experiences, with the intractability of the flesh and the difficulty of living a completely faithful life. Was it also to do with his perception of where Muslim society was going? His programme of universal participation in Islamic religious culture was suited to the days when the Muslims were a small Arab élite at the top of society. The Sunnism that became almost universal in the tenth century was better suited to a time when Muslims formed the majority of every social class and religious culture was dominated by specialists.

In law, Ahmad argued strenuously against the advocates of *ra'y* and in favor of hadith. He did not want to rely on human cleverness to determine the God-pleasing way to live; he wanted to rely on the models laid down by the Qur'an, the Prophet and the Companions. Within half a century of his death, his concept had triumphed, for Sunni Muslims of all the nascent schools of law professed to found their doctrines on revealed sources, the Qur'an and hadith from the Prophet. No longer did anyone appeal to *ra'y*. However, the division of opinion implied by the existence of all these schools of law was not part of Ahmad's plan. Although he did not think the proper use of hadith would always lead to the identification of one precise rule, since even the Companions had disagreed on many points he did not think that anyone ought to base an opinion on what he or any other individual, however wise, had said in the recent past.

Ahmad stood for a sharp distinction between insiders and outsiders, between Muslims and non-Muslims. He chose the creed as his principal means of distinguishing insiders from outsiders, as against the Khawarij, who chose practical obedience. However, he would not admit, in contrast to the Murji'position, that regular performance of the ritual prayer was not an essential part of faith. As Islam became the religion of the majority, pressure grew to accept an average level of conscientiousness. Ahmad was willing to separate a husband from a wife who would not pray or a wife from a husband who would not. Ibn Qudamah, a Damascene Hanbali who lived four centuries later, was expressly unwilling to separate husbands and wives for not praying precisely because it was so common. (Of course, there were no longer any Murji'ah about to crow over his concession period.)

We may accuse Ahmad of incoherence. He kept his distance from rulers and maintained a high degree of tension with the world; yet he also stood on the side of the majority (jama'ah), excluding no one on account of sin. He stood for a highly demanding, austere piety, yet he also opposed special vocations and the professionalization of religion.

The man who would not let Dawud al-Zahiri through the door for having engaged in clever theological talk would certainly not have wished to admit me; yet I must admire him from afar. He had his principles and he stuck to them, whatever their cost to himself – no refusal of moral distinctions or long-term commitment for him. He watched the Muslims around him push Islamic law, theology, and piety in directions he found repugnant, even as they professed to hold him in high esteem. He could see this happening and did not let fame or fortune persuade him that he was the great formative genius of the age.

I have been asked whether I think Ahmad was intellectually the equal of contemporary Muslim jurisprudents. For students of Islamic thought, it is perhaps natural to prefer to spend time with someone like Shafiʻi. Religiously, however, Ahmad strikes me as a much more understandable and attractive figure. For all his penetration, did Shafiʻi mean to affirm anything other than what Ahmad did? The intelligence of Shafiʻi's arguments is impressive but there are also times when his smugness is revolting, particularly when his argument weakens and he presses his case by repetition. I have never seen smugness in Ahmad. It is hard to escape from the faults of our virtues; complacency may be the great temptation for Muslims, corresponding to their impressive personal dignity. I salute Ahmad's humility, above all else.

BIBLIOGRAPHY

This is a list, in alphabetical order, of books referred to in the text. (Note that the Arabic definite article, *al-*, is ignored at the beginning of a name but not in the middle.) Medieval authors are distinguished by the places (where known) and dates of their deaths. Where multiple commercial editions are available, as of major hadith collections, I have tried to cite them in such a way that my quotation can be looked up in almost any. Here, however, I list the editions I have used.

Abu al-Shaykh (d. 369/979). *Tabaqat al-muhaddithin bi-Isbahan wa-al-waridin 'alayha*. Edited by 'Abd al-Ghafur 'Abd al-Haqq Husayn al-Balushi. 4 vols. Beirut: Mu'assasat al-Risalah, 1987–92.

AD = Abu Dawud al-Sijistani (d. Basra, 275/889). *K. Masa'il al-imam Ahmad*. Edited by Muhammad Bahjah al-Baytar. Cairo: Dar al-Manar, 1353/1934. Reprinted Beirut: Muhammad Amin Damj, n.d.

'Al. = 'Abd Allah ibn Ahmad (d. Baghdad, 290/903). *Masa'il al-imam Ahmad ibn Hanbal*. Edited by Zuhayr al-Shawish. Beirut: al-Maktab al-Islami, 1401/1981.

Amr = Abu Bakr al-Khallal (d. Baghdad, 311/923). *Al-Amr bi-al-ma'ruf wa-al-nahy 'an al-munkar*. Edited by 'Abd al-Qadir Ahmad 'Ata. Beirut: Dar al-Kutub al-'Ilmiyah, 1406/1986.

Amwal = Ibn Zanjawayh (d. 251/865–6?). *Kitab al-Amwal*. Edited by Shakir Dhib Fayyad. 3 vols. Riyadh: Markaz al-Malik Faysal, 1406/1986.

Calder, Norman. "*Tafsir* From Tabari to Ibn Kathir: Problems in the Description of a Genre, Illustrated with Reference to the Story of Abraham". Pages 101–40 in *Approaches to the Qur'an*. Edited by G. R. Hawting and Abdul-Kader A. Shareef. Routledge/SOAS Series on Contemporary Politics and Culture in the Middle East. London: Routledge, 1993.

Chapters = Susan A. Spectorsky. *Chapters on Marriage and Divorce: Responses of Ibn Hanbal and Ibn Rahwayh*. Austin: University of Texas Press, 1993.

"Charismatic" = W. Montgomery Watt. "The Conception of the Charismatic Community in Islam", *Numen* 7 (1960): 77–90.

Fiqh = Susan A. Spectorsky. "Ahmad Ibn Hanbal's *Fiqh*," *Journal of the American Oriental Society* 102 (1982): 461–5.

Gibb, H. A. R. *Modern Trends in Islam*. Haskell lectures on history of religions. Chicago: University Press, 1947.

Hanbal ibn Ishaq (d. Wasit, 273/886). *Dhikr mihnat al-imam Ahmad ibn Hanbal*. Edited by Muhammad Naghsh. Cairo: Dar Nashr al-Thaqafah, 1397/1977.

Haththt = Abu Bakr al-Khallal. *Al-Haththt 'ala al-tijarah*. Edited by Abu 'Abd Allah Mahmud ibn Muhammad al-Haddad. Riyadh: Dar al-Manarah, 1407.

Hilyah = Abu Nu'aym al-Isbahani (d. Isfahan, 430/1038). *Hilyat al-awliya'*. 10 vols. Cairo: Matba'at al-Sa'adah and Maktabat al-Khanji, 1352–7/1932–8.

Hinds = *Encyclopaedia of Islam*. New edn. Edited by B. Lewis, et al. Leiden: E. J. Brill, 1960–2002. S.v. "mihna," by M. Hinds.

Hurvitz, Nimrod. "Biographies and Mild Asceticism," *Studia Islamica*, no. 85 (1997), 41–65.

IAY = Ibn Abi Ya'la (d. Baghdad, 526/1133). *Tabaqat al-hanabilah*. Edited by Muhammad Hamid al-Fiqi. 2 vols. Cairo: Matba'at al-Sunnah al-Muhammadiyah, 1371/1952.

Ibn al-Mubarak (d. Hit, 181/797). *Al-Musnad*. Edited by

Subhi al-Badri al-Samarra'i. Riyadh: Maktabat al-Ma'arif, 1407/1987.

Ibn al-Murtada (d. Zafar, 840/1437). *Die Klassen der Mu'taziliten*. Edited by Susanna Diwald-Wilzer. Bibliotheca Islamica 21. Wiesbaden: Franz Steiner, 1961.

Ibn al-Nadim (*fl*. Baghdad, 377/987). *Kitâb al-Fihrist*. Edited by Gustav Flügel, with Johannes Roedigger and August Mueller. Leipzig: F. C. W. Vogel, 1872.

Ibn Hani' al-Naysaburi (d. Baghdad, 275/888–9). *Masa'il al-imam Ahmad ibn Hanbal*. Edited by Zuhayr al-Shawish. 2 vols. Beirut: al-Maktab al-Islami, 1400.

Ibn Kathir (d. Damascus, 774/1373). *Al-Bidayah wa-al-nihayah*. 14 vols. Cairo: Matba'at al-Sa'adah, 1932–9.

Ibn Qutaybah (d. Baghdad, 276/889?). *Ta'wil mushkil al-Qur'an*. Edited by Ahmad Saqr. Cairo: 'Isa al-Babi al-Halabi wa-Shuraka'uh, 1373/1954.

Ibn Sa'd (d. Baghdad, 230/845). Roman = *Biographien*. Edited by Eduard Sachau et al. 9 vols. in 15. Leiden: E. J. Brill, 1904–40. *Italic* = *al-Tabaqat al-kubra*. 8 vols. + index. Beirut: Dar Sadir, 1957–68. The Beirut edition is merely a pirate reprint of the Leiden without the textual apparatus but, unlike the Leiden edition, it remains in print.

'Ilal = Ahmad ibn Hanbal (i.e. 'Abd Allah ibn Ahmad). Roman = *Al-'Ilal wa-ma'rifat al-rijal*. Edited by Wasi Allah ibn Muhammad 'Abbas. 4 vols. Beirut: al-Maktab al-Islami, 1988. *Italic* = *Al-Jami' fi al-'ilal wa-ma'rifat al-rijal*. Edited by Muhammad Husam Baydun. 2 vols. Beirut: Mu'assasat al-Kutub al-Thaqafiyah, 1410/1990. The earlier edition is superior but out of print.

I'lam = Ibn Qayyim al-Jawziyah (d. Damascus, 751/1350). *I'lam al-muwaqqi'in*. Edited by Muhammad 'Abd al-Salam Ibrahim. 4 vols. Beirut: Dar al-Kutub al-'Ilmiyah, 1411/1991.

'Ilm = Abu Khaythamah (d. 234/849). *Kitab al-'Ilm*. Edited by

Muhammad Nasir al-Albani. Beirut: al-Maktab al-Islami, 1403/1983.

Imamah = *Masa'il al-imamah*. Pages 9–70 of *Frühe mu'tazilitische Häresiographie*. Edited by Josef van Ess. Beiruter Texte und Studien 2. Beirut: Orient-Institut der Deutschen Morgen- ländische Gesellschaft, 1971. Van Ess attributed this text to Nashi' al-Akbar (d. Old Cairo, 293/905–6), but Wilferd Madelung has argued for attributing it rather to Ja'far ibn Harb (d. Baghdad, 236/850–1).

Itraf = Ibn Hajar (d. Cairo, 852/1449). *Atraf* Musnad *al-imam Ahmad ibn Hanbal al-musamma Itraf al-musnid al-mu'tali bi- atraf al-musnad al-hanbali*. Edited by Zuhayr ibn Nasir al- Nasir. 10 vols. Damascus: Dar Ibn Kathir and Dar al-Kalim, 1414/1993.

Jami' see under *'Ilal*.

Jarh = Ibn Abi Hatim (d. Ray, 327/938). *Kitab al-Jarh wa- al-ta'dil*. 9 vols. Hyderabad: Jam'iyat Da'irat al-Ma'arif al-'Uthmaniyah, 1360–71. Reprinted Beirut: Dar Ihya' al-Turath al-'Arabi, n.d.

Kawsaj, Ishaq ibn Mansur (d. Nishapur, 251/865). *Masa'il al-imam Ahmad ibn Hanbal wa-Ishaq ibn Rahawayh*. Edited by Abu al-Husayn Khalid ibn Mahmud al-Rabat, Wi'am al- Hawshi, and Jum'ah Fathi. 2 vols. Riyadh: Dar al-Hijrah, 1425/2004.

Khalili (d. Qazvin? 446/1055). *Al-Irshad fi ma'rifat 'ulama' al-hadith*. Abridged by al-Silafi (d. Alexandria, 576/1180). Edited by 'Amir Ahmad Haydar. Mecca: al-Shamiyah, 1414/1993.

Khallal, Abu Bakr. *Al-Sunnah*. Edited by 'Atiyah ibn 'Atiq al- Zahrani. 5 vols. in 2. Riyadh: Dar al-Rayah, 1415/1994.

Kifayah = al-Khatib al-Baghdadi (d. Baghdad, 463/1071). *Kitab al-Kifayah fi 'ilm al-riwayah*. Hyderabad: Idarat Jam'iyat Da'irat al-Ma'arif al-'Uthmaniyah, 1357.

KMT = al-Fasawi (d. Basra, 277/890). *Kitab al-Ma'rifah wa-al-tarikh*. Edited by Akram Diya' al-'Umari. 4 vols. 3rd edition. Medina: Maktabat al-Dar, 1410/1989. The best of four editions from 'Umari.

Laoust, Henri. "Les premières professions de foi hanbalites." *Mélanges Louis Massignon*. 3 vols. Damascus: Institut Français de Damas, 1957. 3:7–35.

Lisan = Ibn Hajar. *Lisan al-Mizan*. 7 vols. Hyderabad: Majlis Da'irat al-Ma'arif, 1329–31. Reprinted Beirut: Mu'assasat al-A'lami, 1406/1986.

Madkhal = 'Abd al-Qadir ibn Badran. *Al-Madkhal ila madh-hab al-imam Ahmad ibn Hanbal*. Edited by 'Abd Allah ibn 'Abd al-Muhsin al-Turki. Beirut: Mu'assasat al-Risalah, 1401/1981.

Manaqib = Ibn al-Jawzi (d. Baghdad, 597/1201). *Manaqib al-imam Ahmad ibn Hanbal*. Roman = edited by Muhammad Amin al-Khanji al-Kutubi. Cairo: Matba'at al-Sa'adah, 1349. *Italic* = edited by 'Abd Allah ibn 'Abd al-Muhsin al-Turki and 'Ali Muhammad 'Umar. Cairo: Maktabat al-Khanji, 1979. Repr. Cairo: Hajr, 1409/1988.

Mughni = Ibn Qudamah al-Maqdisi (d. Damascus, 620/1223). *Al-Mughni*. Edited by 'Abd Allah ibn 'Abd al-Muhsin al-Turki and 'Abd al-Fattah Muhammad al-Hulw. 15 vols. Cairo: Hajr, 1406–11/1986–90.

Muhaddith = al-Ramahurmuzi (d. Ramahurmuz, c. 360/970–1). *Al-Muhaddith al-fasil bayna al-rawi wa-al-wa'i*. Edited by Muhammad 'Ajjaj al-Khatib. Beirut: Dar al-Fikr, 1391/1971.

Mu'jam = 'Amir Hasan Sabri. *Mu'jam shuyukh al-imam Ahmad ibn Hanbal fi al-Musnad*. Beirut: Dar al-Basha'ir al-Islamiyah, 1413/1993.

Muranyi, Miklos. *Ein altes Fragment medinensischer Jurisprudenz aus Qairawan. Aus dem* Kitab al-Haǧǧ *des 'Abd al-'Aziz b. 'Abd*

Allah b. Abi Salama al-Maǧišun (st. 164/780–81). Abhandlungen für die Kunde des Morgenlandes XLVII, 3. Wiesbaden: Franz Steiner, 1985.

Musnad. Roman = *Musnad imam al-muhaddithin wa-al-qudwah fi al-zuhd wa-al-wara'*. 6 vols. Cairo: al-Matba'ah al-Maymaniyah, 1313. Italic = *Musnad al-imam Ahmad ibn Hanbal*. Edited by Shu'ayb al-Arna'ût, et al. 50 vols. Beirut: Mu'assasat al-Risalah, 1413–21/1993–2001.

Muw. 'Ali = Malik (d. Medina, 179/795). *Al-Muwatta'*. Recension of 'Ali ibn Ziyad. Edited by Muhammad al-Shadhili al-Nayfar. Beirut: Dar al-Gharb al-Islami, 1980.

Muw. Yahya = Malik. *Al-Muwatta'*. Recension of Yahya ibn Yahya. Edited by Muhammad Fu'ad 'Abd al-Baqi. 2 vols. Cairo: Dar Ihya' al-Kutub al-'Arabiyah, 1951. Reprinted n.d.

Radd = Ahmad ibn Hanbal (attrib.). *K. al-Radd 'ala al-jahmiyah wa-al-zanadiqah*. Edited by 'Abd al-Rahman 'Umayrah. Riyadh: Dar al-Liwa', 1397/1977.

Salih ibn Ahmad (d. Isfahan, 266/880?). *Masa'il al-imam Ahmad ibn Hanbal*. Edited by Tariq ibn 'Awad [*sic*] Allah ibn Muhammad. Riyadh: Dar al-Watan, 1420/1999. Earlier edited by Fadl al-Rahman Din Muhammad. 3 vols. Delhi: al-Dar al-'Ilmiyah, 1408/1988.

Schoeler, Gregor. "Die Frage der schriftlichen oder mündlichen-überlieferung der Wissenschaften im frühen Islam," *Der Islam* 62 (1985): 201–30.

Shirazi = Abu Ishaq al-Shirazi (d. Baghdad, 476/1083). *Tabaqat al-fuqaha'*. Edited by Ihsan 'Abbas. Beirut: Dar al-Ra'id al-'Arabi, 1970.

Sirah = Salih ibn Ahmad. *Sirat al-imam Ahmad ibn Hanbal*. Edited by Fu'ad 'Abd al-Mun'im Ahmad. Alexandria: Mu'assasat Shabab al-Jami'ah, 1984.

Siyar = al-Dhahabi (d. Damascus, 748/1348?). *Siyar a'lam al-*

nubala'. Edited by Shu'ayb al-Arna'ut, et al. 25 vols. Beirut: Mu'assasat al-Risalah, 1401–9/1981–8.

Speight, R. Marston. "A Look at Variant Readings in the *hadith*," *Der Islam* 77 (2000): 169–79.

Sunnah = 'Abd Allah ibn Ahmad. *Al-Sunnah*. Roman = Mecca: al-Matba'ah al-Salafiyah, 1349. *Italic* = edited by Abu Hajir Muhammad al-Sa'id ibn Basyuni Zaghlul. Beirut: Dar al-Kutub al-'Ilmiyah, 1414/1994.

Tabari (d. Baghdad, 310/923). *Annales*. Edited by M. J. de Goeje et al. 3 vols. in 15. Leiden: E. J. Brill, 1879–1901. Marginal cross-references make it easy to find any given passage in the 1960s Egyptian edition of Muhammad Abu al-Fadl Ibrahim and the 1985–97 English translation from SUNY Press.

Tahdhib = Ibn Hajar. *Kitab Tahdhib al-Tahdhib*. 12 vols. Hydera-bad: Majlis Da'irat al-Ma'arif al-Nizamiyah, 1325–7. Reprinted Beirut: Dar Sadir, n.d.

Talbis = Ibn al-Jawzi. *Talbis Iblis*. Edited by 'Isam Faris al-Har-astani. Beirut: al-Maktab al-Islami, 1414/1994.

TB = al-Khatib al-Baghdadi. *Tarikh Baghdad*. 14 vols. Cairo: Maktabat al-Khanji, 1349/1931. Reprinted Cairo: Maktabat al-Khanji and Beirut: Dar al-Fikr, n.d.

TI = Dhahabi. *Tarikh al-islam*. Edited by 'Umar 'Abd al-Salam Tadmuri. 52 vols. Beirut: Dar al-Kitab al-'Arabi, 1407–21/1987–2000. Vol. 15 covers A.H. 211–20, 18 A.H. 241–50, 19 A.H. 251–60.

TMD = Ibn 'Asakir (d. Damascus, 571/1176). *Tarikh Madi-nat Dimashq*. Edited by Muhibb al-Din Abu Sa'id 'Umar ibn Gharamah al-'Amrawi. 65 vols. Beirut: Dar al-Fikr, 1415/1995.

'Uqayli (d. Hijaz, 322/934). *Kitab al-Du'afa' al-kabir*. Edited by 'Abd al-Mu'ti Amin Qal'aji. 4 vols. Beirut: Dar al-Kutub al-'Ilmiyah, 1404/1984.

'Uyun = Ibn Qutaybah. *'Uyun al-akhbar*. 4 vols. Cairo: Dar al-Kutub al-Misriyah, 1343–6/1925–30.

Waki' (d. Baghdad, 306/918). *Akhbar al-qudah*. Edited by 'Abd al-'Aziz Mustafa al-Maraghi. 3 vols. Cairo: Matba'at al-Istiqamah, 1366–9/1947–50.

Wara' = Abu Bakr al-Marrudhi (d. 275/888). Roman = *Kitab al-Wara'*. Edited by Muhammad Sayyid Basyuni Zaghlul. Beirut: Dar al-Kitab al-'Arabi, 1409/1988. *Italic* = *Kitab al-Wara'*. Edited by Zaynab Ibrahim al-Qarut. Beirut: Dar al-Kutub al-'Ilmiyah, 1403/1983.

Watt, W. Montgomery. *The Formative Period of Islamic Thought*. Edinburgh: University Press, 1973.

Zuhd = Ahmad ibn Hanbal (i.e. 'Abd Allah ibn Ahmad). *Al-Zuhd*. Roman = Mecca: Matba'at Umm al-Qura, 1357. Reprinted Beirut: Dar al-Kutub al-'Ilmiyah, 1396/1976. *Italic* = *al-Zuhd*. Reprinted Beirut: Dar al-Kutub al-'Ilmiyah, 1403/1983.

SUGGESTIONS FOR FURTHER READING

Abu Zahrah. *Ibn Hanbal: hayatuhu wa-'asruhu wa-fiqhuh*. Cairo: Dar al-Fikr al-'Arabi, n.d. Still altogether the best modern study in Arabic.

Cook, Michael. *Commanding Right and Forbidding Wrong in Islamic Thought*. Cambridge: University Press, 2000. Chapter 5 is a wonderful account of Ahmad's moral and social world.

Cooperson, Michael. *Classical Arabic Biography: The Heirs of the Prophets in the Age of al-Ma'mun*. Cambridge Studies in Islamic Civilization. Cambridge: University Press, 2000. Chapter 4 treats Ahmad.

Crone, Patricia. *Medieval Islamic Political Thought*. Edinburgh:

University Press, 2004. Chapters 11 and 16 cover the Sunni traditionalists very well.

Goldziher, Ignaz. "Neue Materialien zur Litteratur des Ueberlieferungswesens bei den Muhammedanern," *Zeitschrift der Deutschen Morgenländischen Gesellschaft* 50 (1896): 465–506. An excellent study of the *Musnad*.

Hurvitz, Nimrod. *The Formation of Hanbalism: Piety into Power*. Culture and Civilisation in the Middle East. London: Routledge Curzon, 2002. Good on Ahmad's social circle.

Jad'an, Fahmi. *Al-Mihnah*. Amman: Dar al-Shuruq, 1989. An excellent collection of the evidence.

Laoust, Henri. "Le Hanbalisme sous le califat de Baghdad (241/855–656/1258)," *Revue des études islamiques* 27 (1959): 67–128.

—— "Le Hanbalisme sous les mamlouks bahrides (658–784/1260–1382)," *Revue des études islamiques* 28 (1960): 1–71.

—— *La Profession de foi d'Ibn Batta*. Damascus: Institut Français de Damas, 1958.

Madelung, Wilferd. "The Vigilante Movement of Sahl b. Salama al-Khurasani and the Origins of Hanbalism Reconsidered," *Journal of Turkish Studies* 14 (1990): 331–7.

Makdisi, George. "The Hanbali School and Sufism." Pages 71–84 in *Actas IV. Congresso de estudos árabes e islâmicos*. Leiden: E. J. Brill, 1971.

—— "L'islam hanbalisant," *Revue des études islamiques* 42 (1974): 211–44, 43 (1975): 45–76. Also in *Studies on Islam*. Edited and translated by Merlin Swartz. Oxford: University Press, 1981.

Melchert, Christopher. "The Adversaries of Ahmad Ibn Hanbal," *Arabica* 44 (1997): 234–53. On the semi-rationalist theological party.

— "Ahmad ibn Hanbal and the Qur'an," *Journal of Qur'anic Studies* 6/2 (2004): 22–34.

— *The Formation of the Sunni Schools of Law, Ninth-Tenth Centuries C.E.* Studies in Islamic Law and Society 4. Leiden: Brill, 1997. Chapter 1 treats the traditionalist outlook, chapter 7 the formation of a Hanbali school after Ahmad's death.

— "The Hanabila and the Early Sufis," *Arabica* 48 (2001): 352–67.

— "The *Musnad* of Ahmad ibn Hanbal: How it was composed and what distinguishes it from the six books," *Der Islam* 82 (2005): 32–51.

— "The Piety of the Hadith Folk," *International Journal of Middle East Studies* 34 (2002): 425–39.

Patton, Walter Melville. *Ahmed ibn Hanbal and the Mihna*. Leiden: E. J. Brill, 1897.

Sezgin, Fuat. *Geschichte des arabischen Schrifttums*. 11 vols. to date. Leiden: E. J. Brill, 1967–2000. Lists the extant works of Ahmad, 1:504–9.

Al-Shak'ah, Mustafa. *Al-A'immah al-arba'ah*. Cairo: Dar al-Kitab al-Misri and Beirut: Dar al-Kitab al-Lubnani, 1399/1979. Pages 687–973 treat Ahmad. Published separately as *al-Imam Ahmad ibn Hanbal*. Beirut: Dar al-Kitab al-Lubnani, 1404/1984.

Van Ess, Josef. *Theologie und Gesellschaft im 2. und 3. Jahrhundert Hidschra. Eine Geschichte des religiosen Denkens im frühen Islam*. 6 vols. Berlin: Walter de Gruyter, 1991–5. In effect, the standard encyclopaedia of early Islamic theological thought.

Williams, Wesley. "Aspects of the Creed of Imam Ahmed ibn Hanbal: A Study of Anthropomorphism in Early Islamic Discourse', *International Journal of Middle East Studies* 34 (2002): 441–63.

INDEX